The Life and Times of a Cameroonian Icon:
Tribute to Lapiro De Mbanga Ngata Man

Peter Wuteh Vakunta

Langaa Research & Publishing CIG
Mankon, Bamenda

Publisher:
Langaa RPCIG
Langaa Research & Publishing Common Initiative Group
P.O. Box 902 Mankon
Bamenda
North West Region
Cameroon
Langaagrp@gmail.com
www.langaa-rpcig.net

Distributed in and outside N. America by African Books Collective
orders@africanbookscollective.com
www.africanbookcollective.com

ISBN: 9956-791-94-6

DISCLAIMER
All views expressed in this publication are those of the author and do not necessarily reflect the views of Langaa RPCIG.

Dedication

To Lapiro de Mbanga, a fallen hero

Table of Contents

Acknowledgement

No intellectual endeavor is free of humps, obstacles and barriers to be scaled. One can never get into the correct track on one's own initiative alone. In June 2012, I made a fortuitous trip to Cameroon with the intent to meet with Lapiro de Mbanga and talk about his travails in the wake of his release from the notorious New Bell prison. Though totally unannounced, Lapiro granted me not just a warm welcome but also an insightful interview that lasted over an hour in his palatial home in the town of Mbanga in the Littoral Region of Cameroon. This is an appropriate forum for me to express my deepest gratitude to a departed magnanimous man who seemsed to have been more maligned than eulogized at home and in the diaspora.

The onus is mine also express my gratitude to various print and e- journals for permission to reprint portions of the present manuscript that originally appeared under their auspices. Friends have been supportive during the preparation of this work. I owe them a debt of gratitude. My spouse and kids have provided more indispensable support than they will ever know. I remain forever indepted to them.

Preface

Revolutionary ideas tend to outlive their originators. It takes a selfless hero to change a society. Lapiro de Mbanga, born Lambo Sandjo Pierre Roger on April 7, 1957 was a conduit for social change. He fought for change in his homeland and died fighting for change in Cameroon. Lapiro believed in the innate goodness of man but also had the conviction that absolute power corrupts absolutely. He was noted for contending that "power creates monsters." His entire musical career was devoted to fighting the cause of the downtrodden in Cameroon. He composed satirical songs on the socio-economic dysphonia in his beleaguered country. In his songs, he articulated the daily travails of the man in the street and the government-orchestrated injustices he witnessed.

Initiated into the pro-democracy movement of his own accord in the early 1990s in the wake of the launch of Ni John Fru Ndi's Social Democratic Front (SDF) at Ntarikon Park in Bamenda, Lapiro remained steadfastly committed to his crusade against misgovernment, politics of ethnicity, tribalism, corruption, culture of impunity, influence peddling, electoral fraud and gerrymandering. Lapiro was laureate of many prizes, the most prestigious of which is the *Freedom to Create Award*, conferred on him by Freemuse in November 2009 at a ceremony in London.

The Life and Times of a Cameroonian Icon: Tribute to Lapiro De Mbanga Ngata Man is the celebration of one man's vendetta against a cancerous regime that thrives on the rape of democracy and human rights abuses. Paul Biya, Lapiro's pet-peeve, symbolizes inhumaneness, misgovernment and the abortive democratization process with which Cameroon has come to be identified. The leitmotif in this book is the

ix

entertainment of resistance in Cameroon against overwhelming odds. As a songwriter, Lapiro de Mbanga distinguished himself from his peers through bravado, valiance and the courage to say overtly what many a Cameroonian musician would only mumble in the privacy of their homes. Lapiro was an anti-establishment songwriter who walked tall where angels dread to tread. For daring to compose an acerbic song titled *Constitution constipée* (constipated constitution) in which he lampooned the Cameroonian Head of State for tinkering with the national Constitution, the singer was arrested on September 9, 2009 and incarcerated in the notorious New Bell prison in Douala for three years on trumped-up charges. He was ordered to pay 280 million CFA francs (640,000 US dollars) as compensation for damage caused during riots where protesters had taken to the streets, angered by high living costs and a constitutional change that would allow the country's president to stay in power indefinitely. Released from prison on April 8, 2011 he was later given political asylum by US authorities. On September 2, 2012 Lapiro relocated with some members of his family to Buffalo in New York where he died on March 16, 2014 after an illness.

The Life and Times of a Cameroonian Icon: Tribute to Lapiro De Mbanga Ngata Man documents the dissident singer's lamentation on the sorry state of Cameroon. This book is the portrait of an indefatigable freedom fighter who remained unfazed by threats from a despotic regime tottering on the brink of collapse. Lapiro was unafraid to tell Biya to his face that his time up and he should pack bag and baggage and exit the presidential palace at Etoudi. He spoke his mind about the shortcomings of the powers-that-be in Cameroon and the foibles of the cabal at the helm. Nicknamed 'Ndinga man' or 'the guitar man,' Lapiro became the idol of the downtrodden and wretched of the earth in Cameroon.

A meticulous perusal of this book would give readers the opportunity to know the man behind the defiant musical compositions they have enjoyed listening to in the past three decades. This book adumbrates what makes Lapiro de Mbanga distinct from other Cameroonian songwriters who seem to vacillate between opportunism and arm-chair criticism.

Chapter 1 creates a nexus between the theory of oral literature and human rights movements in Cameroon and Africa at large. Chapter 2 documents a scintillating interview the singer granted this author in July 2012. The crux of Chapter 3 deals with the expression of political dissent through the medium of musical composition in Cameroon.In Chapter 4 we lay out a framework on which to do a comparative analysis of the musical compositions of three valiant anti-establishment songwriters, namely Lapiro, Valsero and Elwood. The theme of Chapter 5 is the question of language choice in Lapiro de Mbanga's songwriting. It should be noted that this talented songwriter has conceived a hybrid language, 'le pidgin mboko,' mboko pidgin, or 'mboko talk' that serves as a powerful tool at the disposal of the maverick singer. Chapter 6 fictionalizes the rebel art of Lapiro de Mbanga. Chapter 7 is a compendium of elegies and lamentations for the fallen hero. Instead of a conclusion, this book ends with an epilogue in which we cast prying eyes on the import of Lapiro de Mbanga's latest musical legacy titled *Démissionnez!*

"Lapiro de Mbanga Ndinga Man e mandat don bolè today for Etaz! Erreur or no erreur die na ndos! Waka nayo Ndinga man. We go di follow ya 4 chapters di listen ya mutumbu until we own mandat bolè. We go di mimba you tara! All man must go one day ....RIP" [Sarli Sardou Nana]

Chapter 1

Theorizing Orality and Human Rights in Cameroon and Africa

Orature [1] is fascinating in several respects but the aspect that captivates the attention of the audience is the performing art of the narrator. Groomed to not only entertain live audiences but also to shine the light on individual and collective foibles, oral performers command unquestionable respect in Cameroon and Africa at large where they are named differently depending on their provenance. In the Xhosa-speaking communities in South Africa, for example, the *imbongi* [2] has the privilege of singing the praises of paramount chiefs and other high-ranking traditional leaders. In West Africa, notably among the Mande peoples (Mandinka, Malinké, Bambara, etc.), the role of praise-singing devolves on the *griot*. Griots are repositories of oral traditions and indigenous knowledge. By this token they are often referred to as sages. Griots are considered roving libraries on account of the encyclopedic knowledge they possess. They have profound knowledge of the folklore, culture and mores of the people and are capable of extemporizing on current events and fortuitous incidents.

Although popularly known as 'praise-singers,' griots often use their verbal artistry to chastise, satirize, and make loaded comments about the traditional and political leaders of the communities in which they belong. We contend that Lapiro

---

[1] Oral literature

[2] Composer and orator of poems praising a chief or other traditional figurehead

de Mbanga doubles as griot, entertainer and social critic in the musical compositions that constitute the corpus studied in this book. We have not analyzed all the songs written by this prolific singer. The reason is that we intend to write a second book that will dwell on songs composed by Lapiro de Mbanga earlier on in his career.

In Cameroon, oral performance responds to communal needs in both literate and illiterate communities. Consequently, orality and literacy co-exist as two faces of the same coin. One feeds the other. Musicians like Lapiro de Mbanga and his peers no longer sing ex-tempore; they compose songs in isolation and then perform in front of a live audience. More often than not, the raw material they utilize is culled from a communal font—folklore. Arguing along the same lines Scheub notes:

> With the advent of literature, the oral tradition did not die. The two media continued their parallel development: both depended on a set of similar narrative and poetic principles, and each proceeded to develop these within its own limits ....There is no unbridgeable gap between them; they constantly nourish each other ("A Review", 16)

Such a literary synthesis is feasible insofar as a number of conditions are present at the point of encounter between oral and written traditions, including especially the extent to which the synthesizing artist is well rooted in the oral forms of traditional narratives. It is in this light that we have referred to musicians in general throughout this study as songwriters rather than singers. As Ong observes in his seminal work, *Orality and Literacy: the Technologizing of the Word* (1982), "the relationship between these two media should be construed from a historical vantage point: It is useful to approach orality and literacy synchronically, by comparing oral cultures and chirographic (i.e., writing) cultures that coexist at a certain time. But it is absolutely essential to approach them also diachronically or historically, by comparing successive periods with one another" (2).

According to Ong, a historical study of orality and literacy and of the various stages in the evolution from one to the other sets up a frame of reference in which it is possible to understand better pristine oral culture and subsequent writing culture. It is not just the profit motive that serves as a catalyst for translating orality into literacy. An equally valid reason why these artists translate orality into the written word is to preserve intellectual property that will be bequeathed to progeny. In an interview he granted this writer in 2012, Lapiro de Mbanga discusses the rationale behind his decision to write his songs rather than rely on memory alone: "J'ai mes disques que je vais laisser aujourd'hui; après moi on va écouter."[3] It goes without saying that Lapiro is preoccupied with the historical dimension of what he does as a songwriter. He is aware of the seminal role he plays as the mouthpiece of the voiceless. Oral performers fulfill critical social functions in Africa. Their tales encapsulate the most deeply felt emotions of the people whose lives are mirrored in the narratives. Songs suggest to members of the audience the route to wholesomeness. The quest for wholesomeness is the leitmotif in Lapiro's musical composition as will be seen in subsequent chapters in this book.

Many of Lapiro's songs chronicle the trail of dystopia, disenchantment and disillusionment in Cameroon. In other words, the anecdotes he tells in his songs prick the

---

[3] I have my DVDs that will be my legacy when I am no longer alive. People will listen to them when I am dead.

conscience of perpetrators of social anomy. His songs serve as mirrors of the very nature of Cameroonian society. They are the prisms through which emasculators of social ideals could be seen. Most importantly, his songs constitute the means by which Cameroonians are able to find their own connections with a world replete with unfathomable meanders.

The songs that make up the corpus in *Lapiro de Mbanga Ngata Man: Tribute to a Fallen Hero* take readers into the innermost recesses of their consciences and, by means of their luminous images, cast soul-shattering light into their deepest and most secret places. As Scheub would have it, "storytelling chronicles our great transformations and helps us to undertake periodic transfigurations" (198). At the explosive center of Lapiro's rebel art can be found our most profound hopes and dreams, the quintessence of our own very existence. His songs create a continuum from the past to the present. Scheub postulates that "it is the task of the storyteller to forge the phantasmagorical images of the past into masks of the realistic images of the present, thus, enabling the performer to pitch the present to the past, to visualize the present within a context of and, therefore, in terms of the past" (201).

Lapiro de Mbanga bridges the gap between the past and the present by juxtaposing the regimes of Paul Biya and Ahmadou Ahidjo and the ideals by which each leader stands. In doing so, the songwriter underscores the mindboggling dichotomies that exist between these two men and their governmental modus operandi. A number of salient themes woven into songs enable Lapiro de Mbanga to adumbrate the concept of 'good governance' as seen in the following except from his most recent album, *Démissionnez*:

Trente ans de championnats. You dong composé
équipes Wuna dong buka ndamba for all kain stade
Sep so soso défaite because of over boum! boum![4]

The concept of humanism is a leitmotif in all the songs
analyzed in this book. The term is perceived by the
songwriter as the bedrock on which to mint a government of
the people, by the people, and for the people. Lapiro
contends that good governance results from clairvoyance and
the ability of leaders to connect with the populace. Another
theme that is recurrent in his songs is the notion of
accountability. The singer posits that citizens are entitled
knowledge of how they are governed, the nature of decisions
taken on their behalf, and the ramifications those decisions
have on the collective psyche. The themes of corruption and
dereliction of duty are ubiquitous in the songs analyzed in
Lapiro de Mbanga Ngata Man: Tribute to a Fallen Hero. Lapiro
broaches the theme of cohabitation of good with evil in each
of his songs. Interestingly, this is the reflection of the struggle
between benevolent and malevolent forces in action in
Cameroon.

In a nutshell, Lapiro de Mbanga's oral tales are songs of
resistance written with gusto and savoir-faire; they are
performed with zest. The songs harbor allusions, innuendos,
and metaphors. They provide listeners with new lenses
through which to perceive and appreciate oral narratives
emanating from Cameroon. What Lapiro has accomplished in
his songwriting is create a mysticism that surrounds the trope

---

[4]Thirty years of tournament
You have formed teams
Your teams have played soccer in all kinds of stadia
Regardless, they have incurred nothing but defeat upon defeat
On account of excessive boum! Boum!

of the uncoiling black mamba[5] in Cameroonian oral literature. He is a gifted storyteller endowed with a gargantuan sense of self-accomplishment as seen in the interview that follows.

---

[5] The black mamba (also called the common black mamba or black-mouthed mamba), is the longest venomous snake in Africa.It is named for the black color of the inside of the mouth rather than the color of its scales which varies from dull yellowish-green to a gun-metal grey. It is the fastest snake in the world and has a reputation for being aggressive and highly venomous.

Chapter 2

Lapiro parle: Entretien avec le Professeur Vakunta

Professeur Vakunta: Dites-moi, quand est-ce que vous avez commencé votre carrière musicale? Et que pensez-vous avoir accompli aujourd'hui? **Lapiro de Mbanga:** Merci d'être venu. Merci pour l'honneur que vous me faites, venant tout droit des Etats Unis; ça me rassure que quelque part, il y a des gens qui pensent à moi et ça me donne beaucoup de force pour tout ce que je suis en train de faire. Bref, c'est une heureuse reconnaissance. Ma carrière, je l'ai commencée en réalité en 1973-1974 quand je laisse les bancs d'école, peut-être, parce que j'étais un peu délinquant, je ne saurais dire. Mais je laisse les bancs en 1973-1974 et subitement je me trouve en train de faire de la musique. Il y a un orchestre qui est venu à Mbanga pour jouer; il n'y avait pas de batteur et du coup je me suis vu dans l'obligation comme ça d'être leur batteur. Et pourtant, je n'avais jamais fait de la batterie avant. Donc, c'est un don, un talent de Dieu. Je suis allé faire de la batterie. Et c'est comme ça qu'on me prend dans l'orchestre. D'abord j'étais tout petit; il y avait donc friction. Devait-on me prendre ou ne devait-on pas me prendre? Il y avait deux camps et dans le camp qui dit qu'on me prenne, il y avait celui en chef qu'on appelle Kademchi que j'ai appellé dans l'une de mes chansons Kademchi Kadembo. En fait, celui qui est mon père spirituel dans la musique. C'est lui qui avait fait pression sur le groupe pour que je sois introduit. Et c'est comme ça que je commence par jouer de la batterie. J'étais, il faut le reconnaître, un peu agité dans la jeunesse. Donc, jouer de la

7

batterie, je me dis non, il faut aussi que je chante. Pour quelqu'un qui n'avait jamais appris à faire la musique. C'est comme ça que je me mets à jouer de la batterie et à interpréter certaines chansons. Et ça pour moi c'est très important. Il y a beaucoup de choses comme ça. Je peux vous dire que je conduis depuis un certain nombre d'années; je n'ai jamais été à l'auto-école. Donc, euh, je me met donc à jouer et à chanter. Et l'envie de faire de la guitare m'arrive mais on ne m'avait pas appris à jouer de la guitare. Je vois les autres faire, je prends la guitare. Et c'est comme ça que je deviens le guitariste, mieux je deviens même le ndinga man international, enfin qui est aujourd'hui un ngata man. Donc, euh, j'ai commencé à cet époque-là comme ça. Qu'est-ce que j'ai accompli? Wao! Y-a-t-il quelqu'un qui a accompli quelque chose? Chacun va toujours vers l'idéal. Chacun cherche à aller vers l'idéal et ne voit pas ce qu'il a accompli. Euh, je n'ai encore rien accompli parce que Biya est toujours au pouvoir.

Professeur Vakunta: Alors, l'enfance a été pour vous le passage obligé dans la construction de l'homme chevronné que vous êtes aujourd'hui, n'est-ce pas?

Lapiro de Mbanga: Oui, l'enfance m'a façonné. Mon enfance m'a façonné sur plusieurs plans parce que les choses que j'ai vues dans mon enfance c'est ça qui continuent à m'inspirer aujourd'hui. Malheureusement, ça ne change pas et ça m'embête un peu que ça ne soit pas en train de changer. J'ai vécu dans la misère totale; pas moi mais mon entourage. Vous voyez, je suis presque né ici; j'ai grandi ici. Vous voyez mon entourage. Je suis dans une barrière mais parfois je regrette d'être dans une barrière, ça m'énerve parce qu'on ne devait pas vivre comme ça dans notre monde. On ne devait pas se faire des barrières. Mais regardez les maisons de mes voisins; elles sont différentes. Donc, ça veut dire que depuis l'enfance ça a toujours été comme ça; deux mondes dont un est en haut et l'autre en bas. Et moi, ça m'a toujours dérangé; ça m'a toujours perturbé. Je me suis posé la question à savoir pourquoi moi comme ça et eux pas? J'ai eu la malchance ou la chance d'être issu d'un père qui avait beaucoup d'argent; qui était multimilliardaire. J'étais gâté. J'avais pas mal de choses et les autres n'en avaient pas et ceci me dérangeait. J'ai compris qu'il y avait des inégalités dans la société. Quand je deviens grand, je constate que ces inégalités ne sont pas seulement là où je suis né au quartier mais c'est sur le plan international. Il y a l'inégalité entre le nord et le sud où les gens du nord prennent presque tout ce que nous on a. Rassurez-vous, c'est pas nous qui allons faire une tablette comme ça demain (désignant son iPad), c'est pas nous qui allons faire une voiture mais nous avons aussi quelque chose que Dieu nous a donné. Mais ils nous arrachent ça et en retour ils ne nous donnent pas grand'chose. Donc, les inégalités sont partout mais ce qui m'embête un peu c'est que c'est mon frère africain comme moi; camerounais comme moi qui devient l'instrument du nord pour me maltraiter; je dis qu'il y a un problème. Et c'est pour ça que je rends un tribut ici aujourd'hui aux gens comme Laurent Gbagbo, aux gens comme Ghaddafi, pour leur courage; aux gens comme Mandela, comme Sankara pour ne citer que toutes ces personnes qui ont dit non, il y a aussi une dignité au sud.

Mais quand on descend plus bas au Cameroun, on a des gens comme Paul Biya qui a hérité d'Ahidjo qui lui-même a eu un don donné par les colons, donc aujourd'hui c'est Biya qui maltraite; c'est lui qui ne vit pas au Cameroun; qui n'est même pas un Camerounais. Voyez-vous? Il y a quelques jours, il est allé inaugurer; non, faire la pose de la première pierre; Dieu seul sait que si toutes premières pierres s'étaient réalisées, le Cameroun serait déjà un pays qui est sur le plan de regarder 2035. Ouais, Ouais, on aurait déjà vu beaucoup de choses. Bref, il est allé faire une première comme toutes les autres mais pendant que ses ministres pataugeaient dans la boue, pendant que les familles qu'il avait prises pour venir faire du ramdam autour de lui, notamment les gens du RDPC, venaient en voiture, lui, il est venu en hélicoptère! Est-ce qu'il vit au Cameroun? Pourquoi n'est-il pas venu par le sol pour vivre et voir et que ça lui permette demain de faire quelque chose? Il refuse de voir ça et du coup, il est coupé ; il ne fait rien. Donc euh, voilà!

Professeur Vakunta: Quand on écoute vos morceaux, on a l'impression d'entendre plusieurs voix. Alors, je me demande la quelle de ces voix vous tient à coeur.

Lapiro de Mbanga: Tout est spirituel. Je suis un créateur des oeuvres de l'esprit. Dieu qui donne le don ne dit pas parle de ceci; parle de cela. Et quant à ce qui tient à coeur à Lapiro de Mbanga, ça n'a pas d'importance parce que ça tient à coeur à un seul individu. Donc, la voix ne compte pas parmi toutes autres voix. Vous comprenez, quoi? Moi, si vous me demandez quelle est la chanson que j'aime la plus de Lapiro de Mbanga, je ne saurais vous dire. C'est sûr que si on passe au vote; ce ne serait pas celle que les gens aiment. J'ai une manière de savoir la chanson de Lapiro que les gens aiment plus. Je prends un exemple, je vais à Youtube où il y a certains clips de Lapiro et j'essaie de voir celui que les gens ont beaucoup visité. Je pourrais vous dire voilà celui que les gens aiment. Mais ce que Lapiro, lui, il aime, vraiment, ce n'est qu'un simple individu. Et ce qu'il aime, ce n'est pas très important.

Professeur Vakunta: En 2009 vous avez eu pas mal de problèmes avec le pouvoir en place à Yaoundé. On vous avait arrêté suite aux émeutes qui ont eu lieu dans les grandes villes camerounaises. Pourriez-vous nous dire un peu ce qui s'est passé à l'époque?

Lapiro de Mbanga: Oui, c'est, en fait, en 2008 que j'ai eu des problèmes parce que les émeutes ont eu lieu fin février 2008 et moi, on m'a arêté le 9 avril; on ne m'a pas arrêté, on m'a mis en prison parce qu'arrêter c'est quand on vous présente un mandat d'arrêt. On ne m'a jamais présenté un mandat d'arrêt. On m'a appelé au téléphone; je suis allé à l'invitation par téléphone; on m'a conduit en prison. C'était donc le 9 avril. Effectivement, il s'agit des émeutes sur le coût de la vie chère ici au Cameroun. La grève a été lancée par le Syndicat National des Transporteurs Routiers du Cameroun parce qu'on avait élevé le prix de l'essence et ils ont demandé de faire grève. Moi, je ne suis pas transporteur routier. Je ne suis qu'un simple consommateur du carburant; je ne suis pas propriétaire d'un véhicule. Donc, je ne suis pas membre de ce syndicat. Par conséquent, je ne suis pas intéressé à ce syndicat. Vous-voyez, j'ai mon problème qui concerne les droits d'auteur au Cameroun. Je chante depuis des années et mes droits d'auteur ne sont pas payés. S'il faut faire une grève, c'est dans ce sens que je vais m'impliquer. Je ne vais pas m'impliquer dans un dossier qui ne me concerne pas. Mais on m'a jeté en prison pour avoir être, dit-on, l'instigateur de la grève dans la ville de Mbanga et ses environs. Si la grève avait eu lieu seulement à Mbanga et ses environs, peut-être, ça pouvait tenir, mais il y a eu grève jusqu'à Etoudi devant la présidence où habite Paul Biya. On n'a pas arêté celui qui avait instigué la grève là-bas. Il y a eu grève à Buea, à Bafoussam, à Bamenda, à Douala et j'en passe. Pratiquement dans tout le sud du Cameroun. Il y a que le grand nord où il n'y a pas eu grève. Mais il n'y a qu'à Mbanga qu'on a trouvé que l'instigateur des émeutes c'était Lapiro de Mbanga et, comme j'ai dit, on m'a jeté en prison sans aucun mandat d'arrêt, sans rien, ou j'y suis resté trois moins et demi avant de savoir même pourquoi j'étais en prison. Je n'ai jamais, comme

11

j'ai dit tantôt et je le dis solennellement, ni de loin ni près, participé à l'élaboration des émeutes. Bien au contraire, j'ai participé pour apporter le calme à Mbanga parce qu'il faudrait que je sois claire, je ne suis pas un casseur. Je pense que les vrais combats sont les combats de mes idoles parce que le combat je ne l'ai pas commencé. J'ai des idoles dans ce combat et c'est des gens qui ont gagné; qui sont restés dans l'histoire aujourd'hui. Je suis même jaloux de ces personnes-là parce que j'ai envie d'être comme ces modèles. Mahatma Gandhi c'est mon modèle parce qu'il a fait la révolte sans avoir appelé les gens que venez avec moi. Il a fait sa révolution tout seul; seul comme individu. Martin Luther King, ça c'est des gens que j'admire! J'admire le jeune Bouazizi qui a créé ce qu'on appelle le printemps arabe. Voilà les gens que j'admire! Je suis même jaloux, c'est- à-dire que j'ai envie d'être comme ça. La grève n'est pas en faisant couler le sang de qui que ce soit. Et c'est cette position courageuse que j'ai prise au Cameroun en 1992. J'ai dit oui à la conférence nationale souveraine; oui aux villes mortes mais non à la casse! Pourquoi est-ce qu'on pense qu'il fallait absolument casser les choses pour que Biya quitte le pouvoir? Alors, Dieu merci, on a tout cassé; on a tout détruit et Biya est encore au pouvoir. Qui avait donc raison? Est-ce que c'est moi qui avais raison ou alors les opposants, les amis de Paul Biya, parce qu'ils sont les amis de Paul Biya? Je vais vous dire quelque chose, on est dans une interview à bâtons rompus. On a aujourd'hui au Cameroun ce qu'on est en train d'appeler le G7 et quand je regarde le G7 je meure de rire parce que le G7 c'est les amis de Biya! L'UNC c'est RDPC. Fru Ndi c'est un militant de l'UNC. Quand Biya vient à Bamenda créer le RDPC, c'est Fru Ndi qui est président de l'UNC de la Mezam. Donc, notamment dans le rapport de la création du RDPC pour changer l'UNC au RDPC, le nom de Fru Ndi figure là-dedans. Fru Ndi est, par conséquent, un militant du RDPC! Il est aujourd'hui en G7. Zongang Albert est un militant du RDPC qui a été maire et député RDPC. Adamu Ndam Njoya est du RDPC. Il a été ministre du RDPC. Bernard Muna a été du RDPC. Mais je vous dis que le G7 c'est un conglomérat des RDPCistes qui n'ont pas trouvé de quoi manger dans le RDPC. Ce ne sont pas des opposants. Ils ne veulent rien changer au Cameroun. Leur école c'est l'école de l'UNC-RDPC. Voilà les gens qui font le ramdam; qui font le bruit chaque jour au Cameroun. Ces gens ne méritent pas de confiance. C'est des amis de Biya!

Professeur Vakunta: Si l'on revient à votre incarcération, vos admirateurs n'ont pas tardé à la qualifier de travestie de justice. Partagez-vous leur point de vue?

Lapiro de Mbanga: Vous savez? La justice est faite au nom du peuple camerounais, pas au nom d'individu. Donc, quand on rend justice, il y a des gens parmi le peuple qui la vivent et qui ont leur conscience. Je vais vous surprendre. Je suis en prison, et beaucoup de gens du parti de Paul Biya m'ont apporté de l'assistance. Pour la petite histoire, ma femme est du RDPC; elle est même dans un bureau du RDPC ici à Mbanga mais moi, on ne fait pas de politique dans ma chambre. Donc, il y a des gens du RDPC qui venaient me voir en prison, qui venaient déposer des sacs de riz, qui lassaient des enveloppes à mon épouse parce que la justice existe. Toutes ces personnes ont compris qu'effectivement j'ai été jeté en prison arbitrairement. Je ne dirais pas que je ne soutiens pas le RDPC. Je ne le dirais jamais. Le RDPC est un parti politique camerounais qui existe et qui doit exister. Mais il est géré comment? Malheureusement par les voleurs! Je ne saurais avoir des problèmes avec le RDPC en tant que parti politique. Je peux même aller plus loin; quand on dit pour le libéralisme communautaire, les idéaux de ce parti dans le livre, ça a fait rêver tous les camerounais; ça a fait rêver énormément des gens. Mais rien de ce livre n'a été appliqué! Rien de rien dans ce livre qu'on dit que M. Biya a écrit et que d'autres disent que c'est Senghat Kuo, paix à son âme, qui a écrit, rien n'a été appliqué de ce livre. Donc, je n'ai aucun problème avec le RDPC. Il faudrait que ça soit claire. Mais dans ce parti, il y a des gens à la tête qui acceptent d'aller dans les mafias homosexuelles; dans les mafias des sectes et ainsi de suite. Mais il y a des millions de camerounais en bas qui croient en ce parti, dont malheureusement, le statut ne change pas. Moi, je connais des gens ici à Mbanga qui sont dans l'OJRDPC depuis 25 ans. Leur statut ne change pas. Alors, moi je crois qu'on est dans l'OJRDPC parce qu'on est jeune et quand on grandit on monte. Mais depuis 25 ans ils sont dans l'OJ! Vous comprenez bien? Le RDPC, je n'ai pas de problèmes avec lui, mais c'est des personnes.

Professeur Vakunta: Vos admirateurs vous ont qualifié de chanteur de résistance. Que signifie pour vous la musique engagée?

Lapiro de Mbanga: C'est vrai que je proteste mais comme j'ai dit ce n'est pas d'hier. Mon séjour au Nigéria à Lagos notamment dans les années 80 m'a permis de côtoyer les gens comme Fela Anikulapo Kuti. J'ai côtoyé les gens comme Jimmy Cliff. On dit souvent, dis-moi ceux que tu fréquentes et je te dirai qui tu es (rires). Je voulais aussi me démarquer parce que j'ai commencé à faire des disques à une époque où c'était très, très dur. Il y avait déjà Prince Nico Mbarga qui avait déjà pris l'espace. Il y avait les Oriental Brothers. Il y avait Fela effectivement et beaucoup d'autres qui avaient pris la place. Donc, il fallait que je trouve l'espace pour m'exprimer. Ce combat je ne l'ai pas commencé. Comme je disais, Fela a commencé avant moi. Avant Fela, il y

14

avait Franklin Boukaka, le congolais qui a commencé. Donc, les artistes en Afrique ont toujours été sur le plan de la lutte pour le changement des choses. Mais je marque les camerounais pourquoi? Parce que déjà le pidgin c'est une langue des parias, des bandits, des escrocs. Donc, personne ne pouvait avoir le courage de chanter dans cette langue. Deuxièmement, je suis venu avec un accoutrement en jean-jean avec des lunettes noires. Donc, j'étais vraiment un caïd. Bref, il y a le don et j'ai aussi fait beaucoup de travail.

Professeur Vakunta: Lapiro, je trouve que vous avez banni le mot 'peur' de votre lexique. Je me demande ce qui vous donne le courage de dire les choses que vous dites dans vos morceaux à propos du pouvoir en place à Yaoundé. Les choses que vous dites là, il y a très peu de camerounais qui arrivent à dire ce que vous dites.

Lapiro de Mbanga: Ouais, pour avoir peur de quelqu'un, il faut d'abord le respecter. On a peur de quelqu'un qu'on respecte. Moi, je n'ai aucun respect pour M. Biya, donc, je n'ai pas peur de lui. Je n'ai aucun respect pour ce monsieur, par conséquent, je ne peux pas avoir peur de lui. Je vais vous dire pourquoi je n'ai pas de respect pour lui. Je n'ai pas de respect pour M. Biya parce que, comme individu, non je le respecte c'est une créature de Dieu mais ses attitudes, ses agissements m'obligent à ne pas le respecter. Je ne le respecte pas pourquoi? Je ne peux pas concevoir que dans un pays de 22 millions d'habitants, il s'arrange toujours à ne pas nous donner la vraie population camerounaise. Je ne sais pas pour quel but. Je peux m'aventurer en disant que c'est parce qu'il veut truquer les élections. Et que quand même il truque les élections, il se retrouve président de la République avec 2 millions des camerounais qui l'ont élu. Et dans les 2 millions, on a des gens qui sont morts, on des gens qui ont voté vingt fois pour que ça arrive à 2 millions. Je ne peux pas avoir de respect pour un monsieur comme ça. Je ne le respecte pas, donc par conséquent, je n'ai pas peur de lui. Qui a peur d'un bandit? Qui a peur d'un voleur? Je préfère mourir. Je sais qu'il peut me tuer ici s'il le veut. C'est parce qu'il n'est pas Dieu aussi que je lui dirai "go and find yourself somewhere!" C'est tout! C'est aussi simple que ça .C'est pour ça que je n'ai pas peur parce que la vérité n'a pas peur du mensonge. Je suis du côté de la vérité, comment je vais faire pour avoir peur? Quand tu as la vérité même si tu n'as rien en poche, tu es vantard. "I feel proud!" C'est ça!

Professeur Vakunta: Vous êtes chef traditionnel ici à Mbanga, non? Je voulais vous demander comment vous traitez avec M. Biya que les chef traditionnels originaires du Nord-ouest ont baptisé 'Fon of Fons' lors de son passage à Bamenda.

Lapiro de Mbanga: C'est vrai qu'on dit que les chefs traditionnels sont les auxiliaires de l'administration. C'est pour cette raison que j'ai démissionné parce que je ne veux pas être le support d'un pouvoir que je combats. Mais, Dieu merci, la voix du peuple c'est la voix de Dieu. C'est pour ça que je continue à être chef. J'ai démissionné de mes fonctions du chef de 3e degré ici à Mbanga mais je continue à être chef parce qu'à Banso, je suis Shey. Je suis le représentant du Fon de Banso partout où il y a des ressortissants de Nso. Et dans mon propre village maintenant à Bangoua dans le Nde je suis grand notable à la chefferie. Pour ceux qui le savent, je suis même sous-fon, donc enfant du chef et ami du chef parce que j'ai pris la place de mon grand-père qui était un grand notable et on m'a redonné son titre. Donc, vous comprenez bien que je continue à être chef (rires) même si j'ai démissionné de la chefferie de Paul Biya pour ne pas être son auxiliaire et l'aider à truquer les élections. Non, je suis le chef du peuple, celui que le peuple a choisi.

Professeur Vakunta: Votre morceau "constitution constipée" est celui qui m'a le plus marqué et je me demandais quelles sont les circonstances qui ont abouti à l'écriture de cette chanson-là?

Lapiro de Mbanga: Oh! C'est celui qui vous a le plus marqué parce que c'est celui qui m'a aussi envoyé en prison (rires)! Il y en a beaucoup d'autres quand j'étais encore dehors (rires). "Constitution constipée" étant la chanson qui me met en prison, il est tout à fait normal que les gens de bonne conscience comme vous autres, vous cherchiez à savoir pourquoi Lapiro qui se bat depuis des années, pourquoi c'est maintenant qu'il va en prison? A partir du moment où un combattant est arrêté, on essaie d'ouvrir des enquêtes pour savoir pourquoi il est arrêté, qu'est-ce qui s'est passé et tout. Et on découvre que "constitution constipée," c'est la chanson qui mérite cela parce que comme tous les camerounais j'en avais marre. Vous savez j'ai risqué ma vie dans ce pays dans les années 90. Bien avant l'avènement du multipartisme, qui pour moi n'est pas démocratie, moi j'avais déjà pris sur moi dans mes chansons de dénoncer la mauvaise gouvernance de notre pays. Il faut dire que tous les camerounais en avaient déjà marre. Dans les années 90, lors des villes mortes et tout le reste. Ce qui fait arrêter les villes mortes, c'est la Tripartite—c'est bien pour les gens qui n'étaient pas là de comprendre qu'il y avait le pouvoir, les partis d'opposition, et la société civile. C'est grâce à Lapiro de Mbanga que les partis d'opposition ont accepté d'aller à la Tripartite parce que j'avais dit à ces gens qu'aucune guerre ne finit au front; toutes les guerres finissent sur le plan diplomatique. Mais s'il y a la pression sur le terrain, il faut aller sur le plan diplomatique pour obtenir ce que vous voulez. Et c'est comme ça que qu'ils ont accepté à donc d'aller à Yaoundé, à la Tripartite. Quelqu'un de mauvaise humeur va se demander mais pourquoi est-ce que c'est Lapiro qui dit ça pour qu'ils aillent là-bas? Parce qu'à l'époque personne ne connaissait ni Fru Ndi ni Ndam Njoya, ni je ne sais plus qui d'autre au Cameroun. La seule personne qui parlait au Cameroun et que les Camerounais comprenaient c'était Lapiro de Mbanga parce que Lapiro a commencé le combat depuis 1985 dans ces chansons; donc cinq ans avant l'avènement de la démocratie. Donc, le peuple camerounais était déjà acquis à ma cause. Et les opposants savaient que tout ce qu'ils faisaient marchait parce que Lapiro était avec eux. Et je leur avait si vous ne partez pas à la Tripartite, moi j'enlève les mains parce que je ne connais pas de guerre qu'on fait tous les jours sur le terrain sans aller sur le plan diplomatique. Alors l'une des résolutions qui arrange toutes les parties c'est que Biya devait arrêter en 2011. C'est une résolution de la Tripartite. Alors, il a estimé que parce qu'il n'a plus le feu, il pouvait changer la constitution pour se représenter. Alors, moi qui avait poussé les camerounais à aller vers lui à la Tripartite, je me sens concerné; ça veut dire que je les ai envoyé dans un faux truc! Donc, il est tout à fait normal que je dénonce! J'ai dit non parce que je suis le père de la Tripartite! Il faudrait que les Camerounais le sachent. Les opposants ne voulaient pas aller à la Tripartite; c'est moi qui ai fait pression pour les envoyer à la Tripartite. Ils vont à la Tripartite et s'entendent qu'en 2011 Biya va laisser tomber et il va avoir l'alternance. Cependant, il va dans une interview, comme c'est un mauvais joueur pour ne pas dire bon joueur, il va à France 24, on lui pose la question s'il va encore se présenter, il dit vous voyez, euh, 2011 c'est lointain! Mais seulement il n'a pas attendu que 2011 arrive, quelque jours après, il commence à fabriquer des appels du peuple, les je ne sais pas trop quoi pour qu'il se présente. Quel est donc ce peuple qui l'a appelé à se présenter? Les deux million déjà qui viennent de le voter sur 22 millions? C'est une injure à l'intelligence des Camerounais! Il faudrait que ce soit clair. Moi, je ne suis pas politicien. Moi, je ne veux jamais être candidat dans une élection présidentielle ou parlementaire; ça ne m'intéresse pas parce que j'ai l'habitude de dire que je fais le plus beau métier du monde. Mon frère, vous êtes professeur mais on ne paie pas pour vous voir. On paie pour voir Lapiro de Mbanga, hein! Si j'ai un concert aux Etats Unis, les gens vont payer $30.00, $40.00 parce qu'ils veulent voir Lapiro de Mbanga. Qui peut payer pour voir Paul Biya? Ou Fru Ndi ou n'importe quel politicien? Donc, je suis fier de mon métier. Je ne peux pas quitter là où je suis en haut pour venir discuter les choses en bas mais Dieu me dit parle, ton peuple va t'écouter; ça doit changer quelque chose. Je fais ma part de mission que Dieu m'a donnée. C'est tout. Donc, voilà un peu l'histoire de la "constitution constipée." J'y étais au départ et il fallait qu'à cette arrivée là que je dise mon mot.

Professeur Vakunta: Votre langage, je sais que vous en avez un peu parlé, mais le langage que vous avez choisi pour transmettre vos messages est une nouveauté, n'est-ce pas? Les intellectuels l'ont qualifié de "lapiroisme." Il s'agit d'une langue hybride. Pourriez-vous nous dire la raison pour laquelle vous avez opté pour ce genre de langage?

Lapiro de Mbanga: Non, je n'ai pas créé de langue. Je l'ai plutôt vulgarisée. Dans la vie, il faut être honnête; ça ne sert à rien de vouloir avoir des points qu'on ne mérite pas. Je suis presque né ici. Et pour arriver à cette langue, il faudrait comprendre un peu l'histoire de là où je suis né. Mbanga c'est la ville la plus proche au Cameroun occidental, notamment Kumba. Et le marché se faisait entre les Anglophones de l'autre côté du Mungo et les Francophones de ce côté. Pour se comprendre donc, les français parlaient en français en forçant un peu l'anglais pour que l'autre comprenne et l'anglophone parlait en anglais en forçant un peu le français pour que l'autre comprenne. Il y a aussi des langues vernaculaires. Donc, c'est ce mélange la qui a créé cette espèce de pidgin qui est parlé dans la région. Vous comprenez? Seulement, il arrive que la majorité des Bamiléké quand je dis Bamiléké, il faut inclure les originaires des grassfields du nord-ouest qui descendaient à Douala. Beaucoup s'arrêtaient à Mbanga et s'imprégnaient de ce pidgin. Et c'est les mêmes qui descendaient donc à Douala. Vous voyez que ce n'est pas moi qui ai créé cette langue. Comme j'ai dit, je l'ai plutôt vulgarisée. Si le fait de l'avoir vulgarisée fait de moi quelque chose dans l'évolution de la langue, pourquoi pas? Mais j'aime bien à dire que le pidgin est un et le pidgin est universel. Quand vous êtes au Nigéria vous parlez pidgin mais le pidgin au Nigéria a des connotations de là où vous êtes. Si vous êtes chez les Igbos, vous aurez un pidgin avec les connotations igbos. Si vous êtes chez les Yourouba, vous aurez un pidgin avec des connotations youroubas. Et au Ghana, il y a le pidgin. Au Libéria, il y a le pidgin. Partout où l'on parle anglais, il y a cette espèce de langue. Donc, je n'ai pas créé ça Je ne peux pas me vanter aujourd'hui de dire que j'ai créé ceci, j'ai créé cela. Et pour tout vous dire, avant même que Lapiro ne chante en pidgin, les Oriental Brothers chantaient en pidgin, même si ça n'est pas le même pidgin. Et au Cameroun, Eko Roosevelt, lui, il a chanté en pidgin avant moi. Quand il dit: "wuna lef me I play my life, no so I deh oh," ça c'est le pidgin! Mais le mien est plus (gestures) parce que comme on dit, il y a beaucoup de mboko là-dedans.

Professeur Vakunta: J'ai entendu dire que vous vous occupez de l'écriture d'un livre à l'heure actuelle et je voulais savoir de quoi il s'agit.

Lapiro de Mbanga: Oui, j'ai fait (pause). Est-ce que je dois me vanter pour dire que c'est un livre? Oui, puisqu'on va le lire. Un livre c'est ce qu'on lit (rires). Non, j'ai écrit mes procès. Je n'ai pas fait un livre sur Lapiro de Mbanga, non. J'ai écrit sur les procès parce que voyez-vous, je crois que c'est un document qui serait très important pour les étudiants en droit. Ouais, parce que je sors des preuves matérielles pour montrer comment les juges peuvent torpiller le droit pour condamner quelqu'un. Quand on parlait tantôt des gens qui ont pris faits et causes pour moi et qui ont compris que mon procès était un faux procès, je suis entièrement d'accord mais si ces personnes ont compris que le procès de Lapiro était un faux procès, j'ai envie dans cet ouvrage de leur donner le matériel, c'est-à-dire, de leur permettre de comprendre que voilà, quand on vous disait qu'on l'ai mis en prison arbitrairement, voilà donc les preuves. Donc, c'est ces preuves que je veux ressortir parce que je raconte mes procès mais je sors les documents de justice, les preuves du trafiquage des magistrats, comment les magistrats ont changé les élocutions, comment ils ont caché certains documents où les gens viennent devant le juge d'instruction dire que monsieur on vous dit que ce monsieur n'a rien fait. Oui, si vous voulez le mettre en prison, mettez-le en prison parce que ce jour-là il s'attaquait plutôt aux casseurs; il refusait aux gens de casser. C'est ça que je disais tantôt qu'en 1992 j'ai eu des problèmes au Cameroun où l'on a dit que Forchivé m'avait donné 22millions. Mais juste pourquoi? Parce que j'avais dit aux opposants que non! Vous ne pouvez pas, parce que vous voulez sauver le Cameroun, exposer les Camerounais devant les fusils de Paul Biya, il va tirer! Ce monsieur, c'est un malade! Il va tirer! Moi, je n'ai pas droit d'accepter que le sang d'un seul Camerounais, une seule goutte tombe. Et pour c'est pour ça que j'ai dit que mes modèles c'est ceux que j'ai cité tantôt—les Mahatma Gandhi, voilà mes modèles. Je suis jaloux de ces gens. Et je vais vous dire, pour le combat que je mène et j'aime à le dire à mes enfants ici, dans le combat qui est le mien, je ne l'ai pas commencé, beaucoup de gens l'ont fait avant moi mais moi au moins je vous laisse cette maison. Je peux vous laisser cette petite voiture. Ouandie Ernest n'avait pas de maison. Um Nyobé n'avait pas de maison; il n'avait pas de voiture. Vous comprenez ce que je veux dire? Il n'avait même pas d'ouvrages comme moi. J'ai mes disques que je vais laisser aujourd'hui; après moi on va écouter. Donc, je suis au-dessus d'eux! Et je suis très fier que j'ai déjà beaucoup obtenu! Il y a une école pour les chefs d'états? Moi, j'ai accordé une interview ici quand je venais de sortir de la prison où un journaliste m'a demandé, mais monsieur Lapiro de Mbanga, vous n'avez pas de grands diplômes, et vous voulez gérer ce pays? J'ai dit un, je n'ai jamais demandé de gérer le Cameroun. Je dénonce mais ceci dit, Ahidjo, votre président il avait quel diplôme? Matieu Kérékou au Benin, il avait quels diplômes? Zuma, le sud-africain, il a quels diplômes? Vous appelez quoi diplôme? Est-ce qu'on gère un pays par rapport aux diplômes? Chacun gère le pays là où il est.

Professeur Vakunta: Auriez- vous un mot pour vos fans qui sont ici au Cameroun et à l'étranger?

Lapiro de Mbanga: Je leur demande juste d'acheter mon nouveau disque. Vous savez après "constitution constipée" j'ai demandé purement et simplement à Biya de démissionner. Donc j'ai fait le single "Démissionnez" et qui d'office a déjà une sanction de fait parce que, rassurez-vous, vous allez pas l'écouter dans une radio au Cameroun ou nulle part. Et mieux, Lapiro de Mbanga, je suis interdit de concert, donc je ne peux pas stage quelque part parce qu'on a peur de ce que je vais dire. Donc, rassurez-vous, ça ne s'écrit pas mais ça se passe par téléphone et puis bon Lapiro hein, machine truc. En décembre dernier je devais jouer à la foire à Kumba mais le préfet a dit niet! Même ici à Mbanga quand je suis sorti de la prison, les brasseries du Cameroun ont envoyé leur grand car avec des artistes pour m'accueillir, le sous-préfet a dit niet! Donc, le disque est d'office censuré, je dis à mes admirateurs que qui serais-je ici, comment j'allais faire pour être aussi stubborn pendant 30ans, être têtu dans un combat pendant 30ans que je fais s'ils n'étaient pas là? C'est parce qu'ils sont là que j'ai de la force d'aller de l'avant. Et rassurez-vous le fait que je tombe là parce qu'on m'aurait tué ne va rien changer parce que j'ai des enfants comme Valsero qui a déjà pris la relève pendant que je suis encore vivant.

Professeur Vakunta: Merci Lapiro de Mbanga de m'avoir accordé cette interview. Bon courage! La lutte continue!

Lapiro de Mbanga: A luta continua!

What follows is a free translation of the interview into English.

After spending three years in incarceration on trumped-up charges at the Douala maximum security prison in New Bell, Cameroon's political gadfly, Lambo Sandjo Pierre Roger, alias Lapiro de Mbanga remains as unfazed as before by Paul Biya's abortive antics to silence him. As he puts it, "I have no respect for Mr. Biya; consequently, I am not afraid of him. Who would be afraid of a bandit? Who fears a thief? Dr. Vakunta sat down with the Ngata Man in his palatial home in Mbanga on July 1st, 2012 to take stock of the vicissitudes in the life of an unsung hero.

Professor Vakunta: Tell me a little bit about your musical career. When did you start playing music and what do you think you have accomplished to date?

Lapiro de Mbanga: Thanks for coming. I am grateful for the honor you have shown me by coming all the way from the United States to converse with me. This is evidence that someone out there is thinking about me; this gives me courage to persist in doing what I am doing. In short, this is a happy encounter. In reality, my musical career began in 1973-1974 when I left school, perhaps, due to the fact that I was a little stubborn. After leaving school, I suddenly found myself playing music. At that time, an orchestra came to play in the town of Mbanga but they had no drummer and so I became their drummer. Yet, I had never played the drum before. I believe it's a gift from God. Initially, there was conflict because I was very young and band members couldn't decide whether or not I should be hired to play in the band. In one of two camps, there was a man named Kademchi who stood by me and insisted that I should be hired. He put pressure on his colleagues until they hired me. I have made reference to this man in one of my musical compositions when I referred to him as Kademchi Kadembo. If fact, he is my mentor in the field of music. However, I soon became bored with playing the drum and asked band members to allow me take a shot at singing. They did and that's how I started singing some of their songs. This whole trajectory is fascinating and I can tell you that there are many things I have done like that in my life without actually sitting down to learn them. For instance, I have been driving for many years now but have never been to a driving school. Huh, as soon as I started singing, the urge to play the guitar became irresistible. No one taught me how to play the guitar. All I did was watch others play and took a chance at it. That's how I became the guitarist for that band. Today, I am the Ndinga Man International alias Ngata Man that you all know.

What have I accomplished? Wao! Is there anyone on Planet Earth who has accomplished anything? Each individual is driven toward an ideal but isn't quite aware of what they have accomplished. That is true for me as well. I have not yet reached my goal given that Paul Biya is still the president of Cameroon.

Professor Vakunta: Would it be a logical conclusion to say that your childhood served as a rite of passage toward the molding of the accomplished man that you are today?

Lapiro de Mbanga: Indeed, my childhood molded me. The things that I witnessed during my youthful days have continued to inspire to date. Sadly enough, not much has changed and it bothers to realize that there is no change. I have lived close to people who are miserable. Look, I was born somewhere else but grew up here in Mbanga. Take a look at my neighborhood. I live in a fenced home. Oftentimes I have a heavy heart because we are not supposed to live in fences in this world. We don't need barriers. Look at the homes of my neighbors; they are distinct from mine. So, it has always been this way. We live in a world of haves and have-nots. This state of affairs has always perturbed me. I was fortunate or unfortunate to be fathered by a man who was extremely rich. My father was a billionaire. So, I was a little spoiled boy. I had tons of stuff but other kids in the vicinity had nothing. Thus, it dawned on me that our world is a world of inequalities.

It saddens me to think about it. With age I have come to the realization that these inequalities are not just local; they are global as well. Between the North and the South, there is inequality. Northerners are interested in misappropriating the resources that God has given Southerners. Listen, we of the South may not have the capability to manufacture an ipad like this one here or a car but God has given us some resources.

25

And what do Northerners do? They come and grab what we have but leave us with nothing in return. Inequalities exist everywhere but the thing that bothers me the most is the fact that my own African brothers; Cameroonians for that matter, have become instruments that Northerners use to oppress us. I find this scenario vexing. That is why I pay tribute to people like Laurent Gbagbo, Muammar Ghaddafi, Nelson Mandela, Thomas Sankara, and others for the extreme courage they have mustered to tell the North that there is dignity in the South as well. On the contrary, we have people like Paul Biya to whom power was handed on a platter by Ahmadou Ahidjo; who himself inherited power from the colonialists. Biya maltreats Cameroonians, doesn't live in Cameroon; is not even a Cameroonian. Let me give you an example, not long ago he went to inaugurate, rather to lay the foundation stone of some project somewhere (God alone knows that if all the foundation stones that have been laid in Cameroon where transformed into accomplished projects, our country would be in 2035 today). Anyway, he went to lay the foundation stone like many others before but while his ministers and members of his CPDM who came to sing his praises plodded in mud to the site, Mr. Biya came by helicopter! Do you think this man lives in Cameroon? Why didn't he come by road to experience the hassles that Cameroonians endure on a daily basis? He refuses to see reality and elects to live in fool's paradise. That's why he does nothing to ameliorate the fate of Cameroonians. You see what I mean?

Professor Vakunta: Absolutely. When I listen to your music, I have the impression that I am hearing several voices at the same time. I was wondering which of these voices is intimate to you.

Lapiro de Mbanga: Everything is spiritual, you know. I am creator of the intangible. God who endowed me with these talents doesn't tell me to say this or that at any given point in time. He gives me the leeway to say what I want. Regarding what is intimate to Lapiro de Mbanga, honestly it does not matter because Lapiro de Mbanga is only one man among many others. What pleases him is of little importance. You see my point? If you asked me today to tell you which of my songs were the best, I wouldn't be able to tell you because my choice may not be the winner if it was put to a vote. To sort of gauge the popularity of my songs, I have gotten into the habit of going to YouTube and trying to see which clip has been watched most frequently. That gives me an idea of the degree of popularity the clip has gained.

Professor Vakunta: In 2009 you had quite a few problems with the powers-that-be in Cameroon. You were arrested in the wake of the riots that took place in the major cities of Cameroon. Could you tell me what transpired at that time?

Lapiro de Mbanga: Yes, it was actually in 2008 that I had brushes with Cameroonian authorities. Riots took place toward the end of February 2008. I was arrested on April 9 the same year. In fact, they didn't arrest me; they threw me in prison. I say this because you are considered 'arrested' when a warrant of arrest is presented to you. I was simply summoned to the police department by telephone on April 9; when I got there I was thrown in jail. Riots occurred because Cameroonians had had enough of price hikes and unbearably high costs of living. The strike was initiated by the National Union of Road Workers in reaction to the rising price of gasoline. I am not a road transport worker; I am a mere consumer of gasoline. I don't own a commercial vehicle; consequently I am not a member of this trade union. Their

27

activities are of no importance to me. The only trade union that is of interest to me is the National Association of Artists in Cameroon. I have been singing for years but no one has paid my royalties yet. If I were interested in participating in a strike it would be the one organized by the National Association of Artists. Strangely enough, I was thrown in prison for supposedly instigating riots in Mbanga and its environs in response to the strike called by the National Union of Road Workers nationwide. If the strike had taken place in Mbanga alone, one would understand but the 2008 strike was nationwide including the city that harbors Etoudi where Biya lives. The person that instigated the strikes in Yaounde was never arrested. There were riots in Buea, Bafoussam, Bamenda, Douala, and throughout the entire southern part of Cameroon. The Grand North alone was exempted.

In Mbanga it was decided that the instigator of the riots was Lapiro de Mbanga and like I said I was thrown in jail with no warrant of arrest. I was in prison for three months before anyone told me why I was incarcerated. As I said before, and will say it again solemnly for the record, I did not instigate the riots in Mbanga in 2008. On the contrary, I endeavored to calm down the people of Mbanga because I have the conviction that genuine battles are fought by idols. The battle that I am fighting right now was not initiated by me. Mahatma Gandhi is a role model for me because he carried out his revolution without drumming up support from anyone. He fought single-handedly. I am jealous of people like that. Martin Luther King is one of the idols that I admire. I admire the young Mohamed Bouazizi whose lone battle served as a catalyst for the Tunisian Revolution and the wider Arab Spring. I venerate people like Bouazizi! I am even jealous of them because I want to be like them. Grand revolutionaries don't thrive on bloodshed. And that is the stance I took in 1992: I said yes to the Sovereign National Conference! Yes to Ghost Towns but no to wanton destruction! Why do people espouse the idea that things must be destroyed in order to make Biya relinquish power? Alright, things have been destroyed, things have been burnt but Biya is still in power! So who was right? Is it me or the so-called opposition who, by the way, are all friends of Biya? Let me tell you something, today we have what is called G7 in Cameroon. When I look at G7 I cannot help laughing! What indeed is G7? G7 are all Paul Biya's friends! The CDU is window-dressing for CPDM. Adamu Ndam Njoya pays allegiance to CPDM in his closet. He is a former minister under the ruling CPDM party. Fru Ndi is a militant of the CPDM. When Biya came to Bamenda in 1985 to create the CPDM out of the CNU, who was the CNU section president for Mezam? It was John Fru Ndi. So Fru Ndi is a member of the CPDM. Today he is a member of G7. Zongang Albert is a CPDM party militant. He has been mayor and MP on the banner of CPDM. Bernard Muna was a militant of CPDM. These folks should stop fooling around and come clean! They are political chameleons trying to throw dust into the eyes of dullards! The G7 is a conglomerate of CPDM supporters who have not found something to eat within the party and have pretended to decamp. They are not members of the opposition. They don't desire change in Cameroon. Their turf is the CNU-CPDM school. That's it! These fellows who cause much brouhaha in Cameroon are not trustworthy by any stretch of the imagination.

Professor Vakunta: To bring you back to your imprisonment, your fans did not hesitate to call it a travesty of justice. Do you share their view?

Lapiro de Mbanga: You know what? Justice is rendered in the name of the Cameroonian people; not for the sake of an individual. So when justice is rendered, there are people in the community that experience it and take note of it. I am going to say something that may surprise you: when I was thrown in jail, many people from Paul Biya's party came to give me assistance. Just so you know, my wife is member of the CPDM party; she is even an official in the CPDM bureau here in Mbanga. But I want you to understand that we don't play politics in this house. Militants of the CPDM party brought bags of rice and envelopes to my wife because they know that justice exists. They did that because they were aware of the fact that I was imprisoned arbitrarily. I would not say that I am against the CPDM party. I would never say that. The CPDM is a Cameroonian political party that exists and has the right to exist. The question that needs to be asked is how is the CPDM managed? Sadly enough, by thieves! I would not say I have issues with the CPDM as a political party. I may even go further by making the following observation: ideals expressed in the book titled *Pour le libéralisme communautaire* brought a lot of hope to Cameroonians. That book made people dream a lot about the future of Cameroon. But nothing that is written in that book has been implemented! Nothing at all from Mr. Biya's book which critics claim was written by Senghat Kuo, peace be upon him, has ever been implemented. So, I have no problem at all with the CPDM. It is important to be clear about this. But this party is managed by people who are involved in homosexual mafia, occult mafia, you name them. There are millions of ordinary Cameroonians who believe in the ideals of this party. Sadly enough, the status quo of the party doesn't change. I know people here in Mbanga who have been in the Youth Wing of the CPDM for 25 years. Their status doesn't change. I was under the impression that people are in the youth wing of a party because they are youths and climb up the echelons when they grow older. But for 25 years they are still in the YCPDM! You see what I mean? I don't have issues with the CPDM party; I take umbrage at the people at the helm.

Professor Vakunta: Your admirers describe you as a protest singer. Do you see yourself as a protest songwriter?

Lapiro de Mbanga: It is true that I protest but this did not start yesterday. My stint in Nigeria, precisely in Lagos in the 80s, brought me in contact with people like Fela Anikulapo Kuti. I have rubbed shoulders with people like Jimmy Cliff. It is often said, show me your friends and I will tell you who you are (laughter). I wanted to make a name for myself too given that I started producing musical albums at a time when it was very difficult to be productive. Prince Nico Mbarga was there before me. So were the Oriental Brothers. Certainly Fela and others are my predecessors. Thus it was necessary for me to carve out a niche for myself under the sun in order to express myself. I did not start this struggle. As I said before, Fela started before me. Before Fela, there was Franklin Bukaka, the Congolese. This is to say that African artists have always subscribed to the idea that songwriting should be used to bring about change. I have left a lasting impression on Cameroonians with my songwriting for two reasons. Firstly, I sing in Pidgin English which is a lingo spoken by folks living on the fringe of society, bandits, conmen. No one had the courage to sing in this kind of language before me. Secondly, I initiated the jean-on-jean outfit which was quite remarkable at the time. So I was a real caid. In music there is need for talent but one also has to work hard.

31

Professor Vakunta: Apparently you have banished the word 'fear' from your lexical bank. What gives you the courage to say the things that you say about those at the helm in Yaounde? Very few Cameroonians would have the audacity to say the things you say.

Lapiro de Mbanga: Yea, to fear someone you must first of all respect them. You fear somebody that you respect. I for one, I don't have any respect for Mr. Biya, so I can't fear him. I have not an iota of respect for that man. For this reason, I don't fear him. I will tell you why I have no respect for Mr. Biya. Listen, as an individual, as a creature of God, I respect him but his attitude; his acts make me nurse some disdain for him. Why so? I can't conceive the fact that in a country of 22 million inhabitants, he has always managed to conceal the real census figures from Cameroonians. I don't know why he does this. I can only hypothesize that it's because he wants to rig elections. And when he rigs elections, he declares that two million Cameroonians have elected him. Among these two million voters, there are dead people; there are people who have voted twenty times in order to inflate the number of voters to two million. I can't respect someone of this caliber. I don't respect him and that's why I don't fear him. Who is afraid of a bandit? Who fears a thief? I would rather die. I'm aware that he can eliminate me if he wants. But it's because he is not God that I can simply tell him to get lost! That's all! It's for all these reasons that I don't fear Biya. He that speaks the truth does not fear lies. I am on the side of truth; why would I be afraid? When you are a truthful person, you're proud even if your pockets are empty. I feel proud. That's it!

Professor Vakunta: You're a traditional leader here in Mbanga. I was wondering how you handle your role as auxiliary of the administration. How do you deal with Mr.

Biya whom the Fons of the Northwest have baptized 'fons of fons'?

Lapiro de Mbanga: It's true that traditional leaders are considered auxiliaries of the administration. It's for this reason that I have resigned from my position as chief here in Mbanga because I don't want to serve as accomplice of a regime against which I am fighting. I have let go my position as 3rd class chief here in Mbanga. But God is great. I continue to be chief elsewhere. The voices of men constitute the voice of God. In Banso, I have been given the title of Shey. In other words, I am a representative of the Fon of Nso wherever you find Nso people. Moreover, in my hometown of Bangoua in the Nde Division, I am a Notable in the Fondom. For those who know it, I am considered a sub-chief given that I am offspring and friend of the village chief. I have inherited the throne of my grandfather who was a Notable. They bestowed his title upon me. So, you see why I say I continue to be chief even if I have resigned from the chiefdom of Mr. Paul Biya in order to not be his accomplice in electoral fraud and gerrymandering (laugher). I am the people's chief; the chief that the people have enthroned.

Professor Vakunta: Your piece titled "constitution constipée" is the one that I love best. I was wondering what circumstances led to the composition of that song.

Lapiro de Mbanga: Oh! It's the song that you like the most because that's the piece that sent me to jail (laughter). I sang many songs before going to jail. Given that "constitution constipée" is the song that led to my imprisonment, it is totally understandable that people of good faith like yourself begin to wonder why it's only now that Lapiro, who has been singing for many years, is thrown in jail. As soon as a freedom fighter is incarcerated, people normally want to know why he has been imprisoned. Like most

Cameroonians, I had had enough. Every Cameroonian was fed up. You are probably aware of the fact that I put my life at risk in this country in the 90s. Even before the advent of multiparty politics, which does not mean democracy, in my opinion, I had already taken it upon myself to denounce misgovernment in this country in my songs. You remember the Ghost Town Operations and all that stuff. What brought Operation Ghost Towns to a halt was the Tripartite. For those who were not born then, it is crucial that they be told that there was a Tripartite in Yaounde comprising the government, opposition parties, and members of civil society. It was through my intervention that opposition parties in Cameroon agreed to go to the Tripartite because I had told them that no war ends on the battle-field. All wars end diplomatically. When there is pressure at the battle-front, people resort to diplomacy to get what they want. So, with this reasoning I convinced them to go to the Tripartite in Yaounde. Some people in bad faith would ask why opposition parties would wait for Lapiro to tell them to go to the Tripartite. My response to that question is that at that time, no one knew Fru Ndi, or Ndam Njoya or any of the other folks in the opposition in Cameroon. The only person who had the attention of Cameroonians at that time was Lapiro de Mbanga. Lapiro had started this fight for freedom since 1985 in his musical compositions, we are talking five years before the institutionalization of multiparty politics. Thus, the people of Cameroon already knew where I was coming from. Members of the opposition were cognizant of the fact that what they were doing had traction only because Lapiro stood behind them. I told them that if they were not prepared to go to the Tripartite, I would wash my hands because I don't know of a war that ever ended in the battle-field. One resolution that resulted from the Tripartite that sat well with the opposition was the agreement that Mr. Biya would leave power in 2011. But Biya reneged on this agreement. He amended the Constitution and stood for elections. Now, I feel bad because it was me who had urged the opposition to go to the Tripartite. I thought they would conclude that I had lured them into a raw deal. I found myself in the obligation to denounce Biya's volte-face. I said no to Biya because I viewed myself as the founding father of the Tripartite. Cameroonians must know this. The opposition did not want to be part of the Tripartite. It was I who pressured them to go. They left the Tripartite knowing that Biya would not stand for elections in 2011. However, being the sly that he is, Biya granted an interview on France 24 where a journalist asked him if he was going to stand for presidential election in 2011. His response was, "you know, 2011 is still far away!" However, upon his return home, he didn't even wait for 2011 to begin fabricating phony calls from Cameroonians asking him to run again. Who are these Cameroonians that asked him to run again? The two million out of a total of twenty-two million people who had just voted him into office? I saw this act an insult to Cameroonians! Let this be very clear! I am not a politician. My ambition is not be candidate for presidential or parliamentary elections. I am not interested in all that. Do you know why? That's because I have often said to folks that my profession is the best in the world.

My brother, you're a professor but no one pays to see you. People pay to see Lapiro de Mbanga. Hein! If I organized a concert in the United States of America today, people would pay $30.00 or $40.00 to see me. Who pays money to see Paul Biya or Fru Ndi, or any other Cameroonian politician? That's why I am very proud of what I do. I cannot stoop down from where I am on a high pedestal to haggle with folks who are far below me. God tells me to speak because He knows that my people will listen to me. My message will change something. I am only trying to accomplish my part of the mission that God has assigned me. That's all! In a nutshell, that is the genesis of the piece titled "constitution constipée." I was there in the beginning and deem it necessary to have my say in the end.

Professor Vakunta: I know you've already said something about this but I find that the language you've chosen as a medium of expression in your lyrics is a novelty, right? Intellectuals have described your diction as "lapiroism." It's a hybrid language of sorts. I was wondering why you opted for this kind of language.

Lapiro de Mbanga: No, I have not created a language. Rather, I have popularized it. In life, you have to be honest. It does no one any good to try to earn points that they don't deserve. I was raised here. To understand the rationale behind my language choice, it would be necessary to retrace the history of the town of Mbanga. Mbanga is the closest town to Anglophone Cameroon, especially Kumba. In bygone days, there was trade between Anglophones and Francophones on either side of the Mungo. In order to be understood by Anglophones, Francophones spoke French with a sprinkling of English and native tongue words. In a similar vein, Anglophones spoke English adulterated with French and vernacular language words in order to sound intelligible to Francophones. It is this language mixing that accounts for the kind of pidgin that is spoken in the region. You see what I mean? On their way to Douala, most people from the grassfields, mostly the Bamileke and folks from the Northwest, stopped over in Mbanga and immersed themselves in pidgin. So, I did not create this language; I simply made it popular. Well, if the fact that I have used it widely in my songs has made me one of its promoters, why not? But I always let people know that pidgin is universal. In Nigeria people speak pidgin with borrowings from regional languages. Igbos speak Pidgin with words culled from Igbo. Yorubas speak Pidgin with Yoruba connotations. Pidgin is spoken in Ghana and Liberia. Wherever the English language is spoken there is this code-switching. As you can see for yourself, I am not the creator of Pidgin English. I take no credit for being the creator of this language. As a matter of fact, even before I started singing in Pidgin, the Oriental Brothers band has sung in pidgin, even if it was a different kind of pidgin. In Cameroon, Eko Roosevelt sang in Pidgin before me. When he says, "Wuna leaf me I play my life, no so a de oh," that's pidgin. But mine is (hand gestures) different because as one would have it, there is a lot of mboko talk inside my music.

Professor Vakunta: You're very modest. I learned that you're busy writing a book, and I was wondering what the book was all about?

Lapiro de Mbanga: Yea, I did (pause). Okay, do I really have to boast about reading a book? Yes, given that it's going to be read, it is a book given that a book is a document that people read (laughter). I am writing about my trial in court. I am not writing a book on Lapiro de Mbanga. No. I am writing a book on my court trial because I believe this is a document that would be very useful for law students, you know? Yeah! In my book, I produce concrete evidence to show how court judges can turn the law on its head and sentence a person wrongfully. A while ago you talked about people who had decried the illegality of my imprisonment. I totally agree with you on that point. In my book, I want to give these people concrete evidence that proves that my trial was a farce. This book sheds light on the judicial trafficking that is rampant in Cameroon. I want to provide evidence to buttress the fact that judges concealed important documents during my trial in order to incriminate me. Witnesses came forward and said to the presiding judge: "Sir, this man has done nothing wrong .If you want to throw him in jail, do so but know that on the day he was arrested, he was actually stopping people from breaking things up. It is for this reason that I told you a while ago that in 1992, I had problems because it was alleged that Forchivé had given me the sum of 22 million CFA francs. What was the origin of this rumor? Well, because I had told members of the opposition that I wasn't going to condone violence. Just because you want to salvage Cameroon, you do not have to put the lives of Cameroonians in harm's way by exposing them to the guns of Mr. Biya's guns. He will order his fellows to shoot. That man is mentally unstable! He will shoot! I don't condone the spilling of a single drop of Cameroonian blood. It is for this reason that I told you a while ago that my role models are people like Mahatma Gandhi. I am jealous of people like that. I will say this to you: I didn't start this fight. I have told my kids that the battle I am fighting today did not start with me. I have predecessors. At least I can leave them this house. I can leave behind this small car for them. Ouandié did not have a house. Um Nyobé did not have a house; he had no car. You see what I mean? He didn't even have works like me. I have my musical compositions that my children will inherit. After I am gone, people will continue to listen to my music. So I have accomplished much more than my predecessors did. I am very proud of the fact that I have accomplished a lot. Do you think there is a school where people are trained to become heads of state? When I came out of prison, a journalist interviewed me here and asked me why I wanted to be president of Cameroon with no diplomas.

I told him this: first, I have never said I wanted to be president of Cameroon. I denounce misgovernment. Having said that, I asked him how many diplomas your ex-president, Ahidjo had. How many diplomas did Matheu Kérékou of Benin Republic have? Does Jacob of South Africa have any diplomas? What do you call diploma? Are countries governed on the basis of the number of diplomas leaders have? Everyone governs the country in his own fief.

Professor Vakunta: Would you have a final word for your fans who are here at home and in the diaspora?

Lapiro de Mbanga: All I want to tell them is to buy my new CD. You know, after "constitution constipée," I simply asked Mr. Biya to resign from his position as Head of State in the single titled "Démissionnez!" Let me tell you that this CD has already been censored because you'll not hear it played on radio or anywhere in Cameroon. Worse still, Lapiro de Mbanga is not allowed to be on stage anywhere in the country because they are scared of the things I may say. I want to assure you that there is nothing in print about this censorship but everything is communicated by phone about Lapiro and so on and so forth. I was supposed to do a show at the fair in Kumba during the month of December but the divisional officer said niet! Even here in Mbanga, when I came out of prison, Brasseries du Cameroun sent their truck full of artists to welcome me, the sub-divisional officer said niet! So, the CD is officiously censored. To my admirers, I want to let them know that I wouldn't be where I am today, as stubborn as I have been for 30 years without them. Knowing that they are behind me gives me the courage to forge ahead. I want to assure them that if I drop dead today because someone has decided to kill me, it will not change anything in the struggle that I lead in Cameroon. I have younger followers like Valsero who have already stepped into my shoes even though I am still alive.

Professor Vakunta: Lapiro, I want to thank you from the bottom of my heart for granting me this interview. Falter not! The struggle continues!

Lapiro de Mbanga: A luta continua!

Chapter 3

Entertaining Political Dissent in Cameroon

Introduction

Recourse to oral literature as a medium for self-expression and tool of resistance has made gigantic strides in its evolution over the years. In the Republic of Cameroon this transformation manifests itself in the form of musical productivity and scholarship on the subject matter. Among those who have contributed significantly to emerging perspectives on the discipline are musicians themselves. Cameroonian songwriters are township griots who double as entertainers and freedom fighters. Orality is the tool they wield skilfully in an unrelenting war against governmental dysfunction, human rights violations, endemic corruption, bad governance, abuse of power, influence peddling, impunity, misappropriation of public funds and other forms of dereliction of duty that plague postcolonial Cameroon. Of all the musicians that have dedicated their songwriting to the defense of the socially oppressed, Lapiro de Mbanga is the most valiant. His lyrics are telling. He has carved out a niche for himself as the voice of the voiceless.

Songwriting as a creative art in Cameroon has evolved over time. Several factors account for this transformation. The most salient dynamic is the shift in political dispensation. The dictatorial regime of Ahmadou Ahidjo (1960-1982) brooked neither dissidence nor defiance. Consequently, musicians, young and old, confined their art to mere entertainment. Veteran musicians like Eboa Lotin, Salle John, Manu Dibango, Francis Bébé, Ekambi Brilliant, Anne-Marie

41

Nzié, André-Marie Tala and many others who were in the limelight of Cameroonian musical industry in the 1960s and 1970s steered clear of political commentary. If they did, it was guarded praise for the Head of State, popularly referred to as "Grand Camarade" or "Senior comrade" in those days. The 1980s saw the emergence of talented singers like Sam Fan Thomas, Moni Bile, Ben Decca, Petit Pays, Ndedi Eyango, Guy Lobe, and Dina Bell among others. These songwriters, probably still suffering from the hangover of the Ahidjo era, were wary of political commitment. The status quo took a dramatic turn in the early 1990s when under duress from international role-players President Paul Biya reluctantly gave his green light to multiparty politics in Cameroon following the troubled launch of Ni John Fru Ndi's Social Democratic Front party at Ntarikon Park in Bamenda on May 26, 1990.

The advent of political pluralism in Cameroon has given birth to a new crop of songwriters who are unafraid to satirize the shortcomings of the powers-that-be. Topping the list of protest musicians is Cameroon's maverick songwriter, Lapiro de Mbanga alias Ndinga man. Others include Longué Longué, Kotto Bass, Valsero a.k.a Le Général, and Donny Elwood to name but a few. These protest singers have simply refused to be cowed into submission. As Campbell (2001) would have it, "instead of becoming pawns in the political game, they have used the medium of the song...to mobilize the people" (5). Lapiro, Valsero and Elwood are unfazed by threats from Paul Biya's dictatorial government. They tell it like it is.

This chapter discusses the political commitment of Lapiro de Mbanga and what the singer's political bravado portends for the democratization process in Cameroon. We contend that unlike his peers, Lapiro goes the extra mile in his relentless war against all forms of human and political rights abuses in Cameroon. He is not contented with entertaining by means of his ndinga[6]; he takes the regime head-on by blowing the whistle on its innumerable flaws—corruption, dereliction of duty, impunity, influence peddling, tribalism, witch-hunting, and more. Like his South African counterpart, Mzwakhe Mbuli (1992), who argues that resistance is defense, Lapiro perceives his musical art as a weapon with which he continues to wage a vendetta against Biya's lame duck government. It is noteworthy that Lapiro is not merely an observer of the political scene in his homeland; he actually identifies with the political opposition in Cameroon. In fact, he is a card-carrying member of the most powerful opposition party in Cameroon—the Social Democratic Front (SDF). In July 2007, he ran for the position of mayor in his hometown of Mbanga under the banner of the SDF but lost to his opponent of the ruling CPDM party.

Lapiro de Mbanga's music inspires hope for the millions of hopeless Cameroonians who have lost faith in their government. He symbolizes the power of the powerless. In song after song, Lapiro calls on his countrymen to rise and challenge those who prefer to see the downtrodden endure their dim fate of blight and misery in silence. He believes in his role as the voice of the voiceless. As Sone (2009) points out, "the popular singer himself sees his primordial role as the liberation of Cameroonians from the tyranny of an irresponsible and insensitive government...." (19) He further notes that Lapiro's music is a powerful medium for political activism. On this count, Lapiro de Mbanga has gained enormous popularity as an articulate, fearless commentator on Cameroon's political landscape. He is not only prolific; he

---

[6] Guitar

43

is also eloquent. According to Nyamnjoh and Fokwang (2005), "Lapiro epitomizes the strengths and controversies surrounding a protest musician" (269). He is a songwriter known for his satirical lyrics and criticism of politicians in Cameroon. He has devoted his entire musical career to calling attention to the daily travails of pain, marginalization, exploitation and rejection faced by a great many Cameroonians. Lapiro has refused to be at the beck and call of corrupt and morally bankrupt politicians in his homeland and has instead used his musical genius to plead the cause of Cameroon's wretched of the earth (Fanon, 1966). Singing mainly in camfranglais, a lingo that Ze Amvela (1989) has termed Camtok, Lapiro mixes lexical items from English, Pidgin and indigenous languages. With this hotchpotch, he is able to reach a broad audience in all strata of Cameroonian society, especially those to whom his message of hope is directed, namely, the young urban unemployed, cart-pushers, hawkers, sauveteurs or street vendors, beyam sellam or market women, taximen and bendskin[7] drivers and wolowoss.[8] Lapiro has been nicknamed Président du petit peuple or "President of the down-trodden" on account of the poignancy of his songs of resistance. He has become a symbol of resistance to governmental ineptitude and dictatorship in Cameroon.

Lapiro gained prominence in the early 90s during the pro-democracy movement in Cameroon when he launched his groundbreaking album titled "Mimba we." The lyrics of this song are loaded with significations as this except suggests:

---

[7] Motor bike
[8] prostitutes

You wan dammer you mimba we,
You wan souler you mimba we,
You wan nyoxer you mimba we-oh.
Oh Mimba we-oh, tara!
[At table, remember us;
 When you're having a drink,
Remember us when you're having sex-oh
Oh, remember us, you're our leader!]

Lapiro's clarion call does not end at the doorstep of
political leaders. He extends his appeal to the oppressed
people of Cameroon, urging them to stand up for their rights.
He believes that his compatriots acknowledge their
predicament but shy away from taking action to right the
wrongs of the past. They resign to their fate and refuse to
indulge in bold actions. At the same time, they do not want to
indulge in criminal actions as the following excerpt indicates:

We no wan kick-oh
We no wan go for ngata
We de daso for ndengwe
A beg mimba we-oh, yes tara.
We no wan problème para
We no wan go for Ndengui
We di fain daso garri
For helep we own family-oh!
[We don't want to steal
We don't want to go to jail
We just need to work
We beg you to think about us, boss
We are not looking for trouble
We don't want to go to Kondengui
We are only looking for a means

45

To help our family-oh!]

Fear of the unknown is the leitmotiv in this song. Lapiro suggests that Cameroonians have been rendered inactive by fear of arrest and incarceration. It should be noted that the word "Ndengui" is an allusion to Cameroon's maximum security prison, code-named Kondengui. "Mimba we" is a loaded song; it calls upon the Head of State and his ministers to not turn a blind eye to the legitimate grievances of the people they govern. The songwriter appeals to those at the helm to be mindful of the thorny problem posed by socio-economic marginalization in Cameroon. In "Mimba we" Lapiro admonishes the President of the Republic of Cameroon against ignoring the plight of the downtrodden. Words like 'dammer', 'suler', 'tara' and 'nyoxer' are *lapiroisms*[9] created for the sole purpose of veiling his intention to commit what Verschave (2004) calls "crime de lèse majesté" (8) or insult to the Head of State's honor. It is a composite language minted to communicate to the common people in a language they best understand. 'Dammer' is a camfranglais word for manger (to eat); 'suler' translates the standard French word boire (to drink); 'tara' is slang for patron (boss or big shot); 'nyoxer' is a euphemism for 'sexual intercourse.' Lapiroisms reflect the provocative attitude of its speakers and their jocular disrespect of linguistic norms and purity, clearly revealing its function as an anti-language (Halliday, 1977).

Like most protest musicians, Lapiro drums up support from the rank and file as this excerpt clearly shows:

Nkoululu ah wan tok,
Mokolo ah wan gi ticket

---

[9] Neologisms created by Lapiro de Mbanga

46

Marché Central ah go troweh, heh! heh!
Sauveteurs, ah chakara?
[Nkoululu I want to speak,
Mokolo I want to criticize
Marché Central I will talk, heh! heh!
Sauveteurs, I will spill the beans.]

Because he has arrogated the role of mouthpiece of the underprivileged to himself, Lapiro drums up their support in his protest movement against Biya's despotic regime. These lyrics bear testimony to the disenchantment of the songwriter. He chides the president and his lieutenants for corruption, indifference to the plight of the populace, and dereliction of duty. His song is the cry of a disillusioned Cameroonian whose heart throbs for his fatherland. "Mimba we" seems to be an indictment of Cameroon under Paul Biya. After blasting the president, the musician addresses the economic crisis that has hit the nation hard:

For dis heure for austérité so,
For dis heure wey cinq no mus change position
Yes, austérité da be sei dollar no mus change foot
Wusai we own espoir deh no?
[At this time of austerity
At this time when a dime must stay where it is
Yes, austerity means that each dollar must be spent wisely
Where is our hope today?]

The rhetorical questions that punctuate Lapiro's lyrics are symptomatic of the singer's mental discomfort in a world gone topsy-turvy. He lives in a country where democracy has metamorphosed into demo-dictatorship; rigor and moralization have been transformed into reckless abandon

47

and immorality. In 'mimba we' Lapiro underscores the fundamental ailments that have eaten into the moral fabric of Cameroonians and has caused the deplorable state of affairs in Cameroon under President Paul Biya. He insists that there is a gamut of cankers eating deep into the social fabric of Cameroon under the incumbent, not least of which is corruption. Backstabbing, double-speak and a penchant for vengeance on the part of public officials compound the ailments afflicting the nation at risk[10] that Cameroon has become.

Lapiro has been a notorious political gadfly in Cameroon for close to three decades. He has dominated the musical arena and distinguished himself as a resistance singer who remains unfazed by threats of arrest and incarceration. In fact, he has borne the brunt of his political activism in the form of prison terms. In 2008 following a popular uprising against mounting food and gas prices in Cameroon's major cities, he was arrested and jailed in the notorious New Bell prison for three years. But he remains unshaken by these threats and harassment from the government of Paul Biya. He is a musical virtuoso who uses his talents to sway crowds. He utilizes his guitar to communicate messages that unsettle political juggernauts nationwide. He sees his music as a lethal weapon. It should be noted that in 1992, Lapiro de Mbanga reached the acme of his musical career during the infamous "opérations villes mortes" or "ghost town operations." Sadly enough, this period was also Lapiro's waterloo because his voice suddenly went silent and his fans concluded that he had eaten soya.[11] Others thought he had been a victim of government censorship. As Pigeau (2011) points out, "Ses

---

[10] Title of a book written by Vakunta: *A Nation at Risk:A Personal Narrative of the Cameroonian Crisis* (2012)

[11] Cameroonian expression meaning that someone has been bribed

fans ont estimé qu'il avait trahi leur cause et rallié celle du pouvoir. Une rumeur a circulé affirmant qu'il avait reçu 22 million de FCFA de la part des autorités. Menacé par ceux qui l'adulaient peu avant le chanteur a dû se mettre à l'abri à Yaoundé"(119).[12]

However, the truth is to be found elsewhere. Angered by high living costs and a constitutional amendment that was intended to allow Mr. Paul Biya to stay in power indefinitely, Lapiro composed a song titled "Constitution Constipée" (2008) (Constipated Constitution), in which he describes the country's president as an exhausted man "caught in the web of networks that compel him to stay in power even though he is tired." In this song, Lapiro calls for help, probably from the international community, to stop Paul Biya from committing constitutional rape. He states in no uncertain terms that Paul Biya is burned out and needs to retire without further ado as seen in the excerpt below:

Au secours!
L'heure est grave
Les bandits en cols blancs
Veulent braquer la constitution de mon pays
Les fossoyeurs de la république
Veulent mettre les lions en cage (…)
Le coq est harcelé et menacé d'une tentative de holdup (…)
Big Katika don taya'oh!
Répé don slack'oh!

---

[12] His fans thought he had betrayed their cause by crossing the carpet to join the camp of the ruling party. A rumor had circulated that he had received the sum of 22 million CFA francs from the government. Threatened by those same people who had sung his praises the singer sought refuge in Yaounde.

Wuna lep yi yi rest
Répé don fatigué
Yi wan go rest (…)
Help!
Come deliver us
There is danger out there
White-collar thieves are
Bent on mutilating the Constitution of my country
The Nation's grave-diggers want to
Put the Lions in the cage (…)
The rooster is harassed and shaken by threats of hold-up
The Big Boss is tired
The Father of the Nation is exhausted
Give him the opportunity to rest
Pa is tired
He needs help (…) [xi]

This song is a mix of French and Cameroonian pidgin English. It became the unofficial anthem of protesters during the 2008 youth uprising in Cameroon, and Lapiro was arrested and charged with inciting unrest. In spite of this humiliation by the government of his homeland, Lapiro de Mbanga has regained international renown and has become even more vocal against the misdeeds of the Biya regime. During the presidential poll on October 9th, 2011 he called on all conscientious Cameroonians to cast blank votes to show their contempt for Mr. Paul Biya. In November 2009, he was selected as the winner of the global "Freedom to Create Imprisoned Artists Prize". The jury remarked that his songs constituted a cultural megaphone by which the disenfranchised and politically endangered can vicariously exercise free speech.

The language in "Constitution Constipée" is surprisingly free of the Lapiroism to which this maverick songwriter has accustomed his admirers. However, Lapiro culls words and expressions from Pidgin and indigenous languages spoken in Cameroon to embellish his songwriting. He speaks in a lingo that the rank and file can understand. Expressions such as "Big Katika don taya'oh!", "Répé don slack'oh!", "Wuna lep yi yi rest", "Répé don fatigué" and "Yi wan go rest (…) are pidgin expressions. This extremely brilliant singer has even created his own lingo which is extremely difficult for the elite to understand on account of the lexical obfuscation that veils it. It should be noted that the word "répé" is the inverted form of "père" [father]. Camfranglais speakers have borrowed this technique of lexical inversion from speakers of French Verlan.[13]

In 2001, Lapiro wrote a song titled "Na You" in which he sounded brazenly confrontational. "Na You" is a pidgin expression that could be translated as 'You are to Blame.' Circumstances surrounding the composition of this song are a classic example of the transformation of a social rebel into an astute and indefatigable political activist. In the song, Lapiro bemoans the rape of democracy in Cameroon. As he puts it, "People should make a distinction between multiparty politics and democracy. I think that what we have in Cameroon is multiparty and not democracy. Even within political parties, the assessment is the same because those with new ideas and contrary views are regarded as opposition within the house and if you insist you are dismissed" (quoted in Sone, 25).

---

[13] Verlan is common youth language in France, especially those living on the fringe of society. It rests on a long French tradition of transposing syllables of individual words to create slang words.

In "Na You" Lapiro stands up tall in front of the Cameroonian Head of State, and figuratively spits in his face—or to use the actual language of rustics, pisses on him:

You go for Bamenda
Abakwa boys dem di sofa.
From north to south
Ma complice dem di hala-oh!
From east to west-oh!
Free boys dem di gaz-oh!
Na you do'am —oh!
Na you do'am —oh!
Na you do'am —oh! Heh! Heh!
Na you sipoil dis kondre
[If you go to Bamenda
You'll find Abakwa boys suffering
From north to south
My friends are protesting!
From east to west-oh!
Free boys are farting-oh!
You are to blame-oh!
You are to blame-oh!
You are to blame-oh! Heh! Heh!

The accusing finger that Lapiro points in the face of Paul Biya is as provocative as his words are defiant. In no uncertain terms, he holds the president accountable for all the mess in Cameroon: "Na you do'am–oh!" / "Na you sipoil dis kondre!" This could be translated as "You did it!" "You have ruined this country." The rebellious songwriter does not stop at accusation; he enjoins the president to repair the damage without further ado:

You mus fix'am–oh!
You mus fix'am–oh!
You go fix'am–oh!
Na you demage dis kondre
You mus fix'am–oh!
You go fix'am–oh!
[You must fix it–oh!
You must fix it–oh!
You have to fix it–oh!
You have ruined this country
You have to fix it–oh!]

Lapiro insists on getting to the bottom of the mess in Cameroon and promises to sing the truth and nothing but the truth. It is important to note that Lapiro's lyrics amount to political commentary. His songs are tainted with socio-political realism. Listen to what he has to say about the need for politicians to be truthful to the electorate:

La vérité étant… ce qu'on ne retrouve jamais
Aux tables des menteurs
Je jure de chanter la vérité et rien que la vérité
Mombo ah go brass before dem meng me
But ah go bras daso
Baisse de salaire na you!
Arriérés na you!
Compression du personnel na you!
Licenciement na you!
Privatisation na you!
Liquidation na soso you…
Moi ah comprends sei
Do how, do how Johnny four foot

Go las come dammer nylon ana carton for dis kondre…

[xv]

[Truth is never… found at the table of liars
I promise to sing the truth and nothing but the truth
My friend, I will speak at the risk of being killed
I will speak regardless of what happens to me
Salary cuts is your handiwork
Deferred payments of arrears is you
Employee lay-offs is you
Privatizing state enterprises is you
Running companies aground is still you
It is now clear to me that in the not too distant future
The goat will have no choice but to eat nylon and
cardboard boxes in this country.]

Lapiro's tone is both aggressive and provocative in this
song. In a damning diatribe, he banishes truth from the
discourse of politicians: "La vérité étant… ce qu'on ne
retrouve jamais aux tables des menteurs." He does not only
label politicians liars, but he also pins the blame for chronic
unemployment, salary cuts, employee lay-offs, privatization of
state enterprises and more on the shoulders of politicians. He
argues that if this decline continues, there will come a time
when Cameroonians will have a hard time of it: "Do how, do
how Johnny four foot go las come dammer nylon ana carton
for dis kondre." Lapiro underscores the dire consequences of
this state of affairs as follows:

Conséquence, boys dem dong ton na attaquant
Nga na ninja
Small tchotchoro for quartier dem dong begin
Aggresser man pikin for carrefour…
Licencié na taximan

54

Ala wan na bendskinneur
BTS na secrétaire for long sitik
Someone na bayam sellam
GCE O/L na cuti mbanga wet cuti rubber
Ala war di wan na for farm banana
Breveté na chargeur
Ala wan na forceur
GCE A/L na broke stone
Someone di dig na sand-sand
Na we dis today kondre dong fall stock..."
[Consequently, boys have become attackers
Girls have become ninjas
Little girls are now sexually harassing men at the
intersection
BA degree holders are taximen
Others are bendskin commuters
BTS holders work as secretaries in offices
Others are market women
GCE O/L hoders are harvesting palm nuts and rubber
for a living
Others are involved in manual labor on banana
plantations
Brevete holders are park boys
Others are loaders
GCE A/L holders break stones as a means of livelihood
Here we are living in a country that is bankrupt ...]

What Lapiro says in his lyrics may sound illusionary for
listeners who are not familiar with the status quo in
Cameroon today. But his words ring so true that
Cameroonians with love for the fatherland cannot help but
shed tears. For instance, who would fathom the likelihood of
GCE A/L certificate holders breaking stones as a livelihood

in the 21ˢᵗ century? Sadly enough, this is not a figment of Lapiro's imagination, it is reality. Holders of the GCE O/L certificate and its French equivalent called Breveté are earning a pittance by harvesting palm-nuts and rubber in Cameroon today. Anyone who disputes the veracity of Lapiro's assertions would do well to make a trip to Cameroon and the truth will dawn on them. As always, the tireless singer calls on the powers-that-be to step in and do the right thing by fixing the mess they have caused.

> You mus fix'am–oh!
> You mus fix'am–oh!
> You go fix'am–oh!
> You mus fix'am–oh!
> You go fix'am–oh!
> [You must fix it–oh!
> You must fix it–oh!
> You have to fix it–oh!
> You must fix it–oh!
> You have to fix it–oh!]

The social chaos and economic morass prevalent in Cameroon constitute the central theme in Lapiro's musical composition. His sarcasm and outright invectives are directed at Paul Biya, the Cameroonian Head of State who has been described by French journalists as "Le Roi Fainéant or the Lazy King. [14]The fiery singer does not mince words as he bemoans the fate of university graduates turned taximen and bendskin drivers: "Licencié na taximan /Ala wan na

---

[14] Mockery of President Paul Biya of Cameroon by French Journalists," Retrieved May 20 from http://www.postnewsline.com/2012/04/synopsis-mockery-of-paul-biya-by-french-journalists.html

bendskinneur." In this song, Lapiro de Mbanga takes umbrage at a system that kills its youths; a system that reduces its educated youths to call girls and urchins: "boy dem dong ton na attaquant nga na ninja /small tchotchoro for quartier dem dong begin/aggresser man pikin for carrefour..." What Lapiro says in his lyrics may sound far-fetched but the fact of the matter is that hundreds of thousands of university graduates are roaming the streets in Cameroon looking for odd jobs just to make a living in a country that is replete with natural resources. The musician contends that Paul Biya's legacy to Cameroonians is a poisoned gift. So much for the decay of a nation state! Of all the protest musicians in Cameroon, Lapiro de Mbanga seems to be the most audacious and clairvoyant. He is a visionary. He is fearless. He speaks the truth, without giving a damn whose ox is gored.

In another song titled "Lef am so" Lapiro calls for the arrest of Mr. Paul Biya and his criminal ministers:

> Envoyez tout le monde à kondengui!
> Tout le monde à kondengui!
> Big Katika à kondengui!
> Tous les ministres à kondengui!
> Biensûr! Biensûr Biensûr! (...)
> [Send everybody to kondengui!
> Everybody to kondengui!
> Send Big Katika to kondengui!
> Send all his ministers to Kondengui!
> Sure! Sure! Sure! (...)]

The language used in this song is likely to pose insurmountable comprehension obstacles to foreign listeners not familiar with Lapiroisms. A word like 'Katika' is a polysemous lexeme. In other words, it carries several connotations. In daily usage, "katika" refers to a bouncer in a nightclub. Lapiro has resorted to the technique of semantic shift to endow the word with an entirely new signification. In this song, it refers to the Head of State or leader in Cameroon. In a similar vein, 'mandat' has undergone a semantic shift and taken on a new meaning. It is used in this context as a translation of the English word, "life span" or "existence." "Nchinda" is a loan from Pidgin English. Generally, it translates the notion of "royal page". In this context, it translates the English word "lieutenant" or "minister". 'Ndoh' is a camfranglais (Kouega, 2003) word for 'money'. Njaka and manguru ngwété are expressions gleaned from Cameroonian indigenous languages. Njaka is a Duala word for "child." Manguru ngwété" translates the concept of abject poverty. A synonym is 'ngueme,' used elswehwere in this book.

Lapiro resorts to polysemy and code-switching in an attempt to translate the speech patterns of the people he addresses in his musical compositions. His overriding goal is to voice popular discontent against a regime in a language intelligible to the riff raff. If for this reason that Nyamnjoh and Fokwang (2005) note that Lapiro's music "reveals the peculiar character of the relations between art, specifically oppositional music, and a postcolonial African State" (252).In Lapiro's music lurks the irrepressible urge to articulate, and name the incredible. If Lapiro remains Cameroon's most revered musician, it is precisely on account of his multifaceted response to Cameroon's postcolonial incredibility. He is notorious for the daring punches he throws at the cabal governing Cameroon today. His acrimonious diatribes and invectives are leveled at individuals and institutions he perceives as perpetrators of social injustice. In doing so, he has successfully cultivated and made hegemonic in global consciousness an image of himself as a quintessentially anti-establishment musician.

In a nutshell, this critical analysis of selected pieces from Lapiro's musical repertoire leads us to the conclusion that his music is not only danceable but also didactic. His songs of protest address Cameroon's perennial problems. He calls upon perpetrators and victims of human rights abuses to turn on a new page and make a volte-face. The rationale for Lapiro's musical compositions is to raise awareness in the hope of galvanizing the masses into open revolt. Mandela aptly captures the quintessence of protest music when he observes that African music is often about the aspirations of African people, and it can ignite the political resolve of those who might otherwise be indifferent to politics (*Long Walk to Freedom*, 1994). Lapiro is a protest songwriter whose lyrics harbor seeds of a revolution. His danceable lyrics translate mixed messages of hope and despair. The motif that runs through his songs is the theme of universal human rights and freedoms. His songs have produced a tonic effect on the younger generation of songwriters who are now hell bent on taking their destiny into their own hands by all means necessary. Lapiro is a protest songwriter who doubles as entertainer and social critic. His language could be described as a mix of several codes as the following chapter clearly illustrates.

Chapter 4

Lapiroisms: Language of Resistance in Cameroonian Music

Introduction

Regardless of genre, music performs a myriad social functions; it reflects the joys, sorrows, hopes and despair of the people whose lived experiences constitute the subject matter of songwriting. As Rick Hesch points out, "songwriting may be the one true expression of a people's sorrow, despair and hope" (1). He notes that the Wobblies wrote and performed songs as instruments of mobilization in the early twentieth century. Music and the American civil rights movements of the sixties became almost synonymous, as many African-American musicians, from James Brown to Stevie Wonder, celebrated black consciousness and called for social change. Tayannah Lee McQuillar and Fred Johnson (2010) note that Tupac Shakur's rap songs translate the traumas experienced by Tupac himself and disillusioned African-Americans. His song titled "Holler If Ya Hear Me" from his album *Strictly 4 My N.I.G.G.A.Z* struck a chord with a large section of disaffected African-American youths exasperated by poverty, police brutality, racial profiling and more. In the same vein, the rappers who presaged urban riots in France have proven that social imbalances can provide material for resistance. They see the connection between their experience in the banlieues[15] and that of African-Americans living in the inner cities. Most French Rappers tend to have

---

[15] Ghettoes

recourse to Verlan in their songwriting as a means of masking significations in order to say out of legal harm's way. In an article titled "Le Camfranglais, Un cousin du Verlan?" (1989), Michel Lobé Ewané draws striking parallels between Camfranglais and Verlan. He posits that Verlan was invented as a secret code by French youths, drug users and criminals to communicate freely in front of authority figures (parents and police). The term 'verlan' is itself a reverse-syllable, which becomes l'envers (meaning backwards) when turned round. French musical groups such as NTM, Ministère AMER, and Assassins often resort to Verlan in order to speak angrily about life in the French suburbs through songs that attack the police, the government and the French state. Lapiro de Mbanga has followed in the footsteps of the French thanks to his Lapiroisms.

Musical Lapiroisms

Lexical manipulation is a major feature of Lapiro's use of the French language. Singing mainly in Camfranglais (township lingo), and Pidgin English (Cameroonian Creole), he is able to reach a broad audience in all strata of society, especially those where his diatribes are well received, i.e., the young urban unemployed, cart-pushers, hawkers, sauveteurs or hawkers, bayam sellam or market women, taximen and bendskin drivers. In one of his early albums titled, *Kob Nye*, Lapiro uses coded language to berate Cameroonian politicians for their role in the socio-economic morass and widespread misery orchestrated by bad governance in Cameroon. He identifies with the opposition in Cameroon and has become popular as a result of his outspokenness during the trial of two Cameroonian intellectual critics of the government of Mr. Paul Biya—Célestin Monga and Pius Njawé, both charged with treason and contempt of the Head of State many years ago. Lapiro's diction serves as a smokescreen for veiling the insults he hauls at the powers- that- be in Cameroon. His lyrics speak volumes about the experience of hunger, deprivation, uncertainty in the lives of suffering masses, and the need for the rule of law in his homeland. His songs admonish State officials against turning a blind eye to the predicament of the *petit peuple* or the small people. Lapiroisms are created for the purpose of veiling discourse from law enforcement officers—gendarmes, police and the military. Sometimes, Lapiro resorts to clipping in a bid to produce new words. The word 'milito', for instance, is a truncation of the word 'militaire' (military).

Lapiroism is a composite language minted to communicate to the common people in a language they best understand. Lapiroisms became popular in Cameroon between 1990 and 1992, an era associated with the emergence of opposition political parties. An impressionistic inspection of fluent speakers of Lapiroisms reveals that they are peddlers, taximen, bendskinneurs, wheelcart pushers, hawkers, prostitutes, vagabonds, thieves, prisoners, gamblers, conmen, musicians and comedians. The lexical manipulation, phonological truncation, morphological hybridization, semantic shift, relexification, and dysphemistic extensions characteristic of Lapiroisms reflect the provocative attitude of its speakers and their jocular disrespect of grammatical rules.

This urban slang functions like other slangs all over the world; however it is unique in combining elements from French, English, Pidgin, and Cameroonian local languages as this example from his song "Tout le monde à Kondengui" (Everybody to Kondengui) clearly indicates: "We dong hypothéquer avenir for we njaka forever and ever" (we have

63

mortgaged the future of our children forever). The word smiting in this statement calls for close analysis. Lapiro employs four languages in this single sentence. "We" and "forever and ever" are Standard English words. "Dong" is a Pidgin English word which could be translated as "have" (we dong = we have). "Njaka" is an indigenous word culled from Duala, a local language spoken in Cameroon. More often than not Lapiro resorts to the technique of semantic shift as seen in the following sentence: "Je jure que yi own mandat dong shot ("Tout le monde à Kondengui"). [I swear that his days are numbered]. As in the previous statement, the singer combines lexes from French, English and Pidgin to create a third code. It is interesting to note that the word "shot" has been given a new meaning in Lapiro's lingo. In this context the word could be translated as "short-lived". "Yi own mandat dong shot" could be translated as "His days are numbered". "Mandat" is a French word that means "term of office" or "money order," but used by Lapiro in this context in reference to the duration of someone's life on earth. Another example is: "Big Katika for Ngola and yi Nchinda dem say...." It should be noted that the word "Nchinda" is a Pidgin English word that describes the servants of traditional leaders such as chiefs and Fons[16]. However, Lapiro endows this well-known word with a new signification. In the excerpt above "nchinda" refers to the ministers appointed by the Head of State to serve him, just as royal pages serve the Monarch. The word "Ngola" is the indigenous name for Yaounde, used here metonymically to represent the Republic of Cameroon. "Katika" literally means "bouncer" in a nightclub but has undergone semantic shift in Lapiro's lyrics to refer to Head of State or President. These examples brook

---

[16] Monarch

no doubt that Lapiroisms is a composite language consciously developed by the songwriter through the process of relexification. Chantal Zabus defines this mode of writing as "the writer's attempt at textualizing linguistic differentiation and conveying African concepts, thought patterns and linguistic concepts through the ex-colonizer's language" (23). Moreover, Lapiro employs parallelisms to sound a clarion call for open rebellion against an ailing polity in Cameroon as this excerpt culled from his Album titled *Lef am so* (Live and Let Live) indicates:

Ma complice dem for Mokolo-o!
Ma complice dem for Nkouloulou-o!
Ma complice dem for Marché central-o!
Ma complice dem for gares routières-o!
[My accomplices in Mokolo-o!
My accomplices in Nkouloulou-o!
My accomplices in the Main Market-o!
My accomplices at the motor park-o!]

This passage sounds like the voice of a rebel leader summoning his people to take up the cudgels and battle with the grave-diggers of a moribund nation-state. People listening to this piece cannot ignore the power of repetition that conveys the meaning intended by the songwriter. The esthetic beauty of this song derives from the singer's use of a distinctive rhetorical device, namely parallelism. It is repetition that gives dynamism to Lapiro's songs. Each time certain words are reiterated, the impact grows stronger. For example, a word like "complice" is pregnant with meaning. It could be interpreted as "comrades in arm," "accomplices," or "sympathizers." The word relates the germ of meaning which it carries. Furthermore, repeated words recall the utterances

which have preceded them. As Julien (1978) points out, "...
repeated words have dual verbal signification" (82). The
passage above derives its force and eloquence from Lapiro's
use of parallel phrasing. Parallel phrasing creates an
accelerating rhythm as specific words and phrases are
repeated. For instance, the 'o' in each sentence above is a
marker of orality in Cameroonian discourse.

Language mixing is part and parcel of Lapiroisms. Lapiro
mixes codes derived from several Cameroonian languages.
The technique of code-switching enables him to level
diatribes at the Cameroonian Head of State and his
lieutenants without running the risk of being apprehended.
He mixes Camfranglais words, French, and Pidgin English
expressions for the purpose of underscoring the plurilingual
socio-cultural backdrop against which his songs are written as
this excerpt from "Tout le monde à Kondengui", illustrates:

> Je jure que yi own mandat dong shot...
> Dat be say njaka for njaka for we njaka
> Dem go come boulot for pay dang ndoh...
> Big Katika for Ngola and yi Nchinda dem say...
> Comme vous pouvez le constater,
> Cameroon dong capside...
> [This implies that our great grandchildren
> Shall work to pay back these loans
> Big Katika in Ngola and his lieutenants say...
> As you can see for yourselves,
> This country is topsy-turvy,
> Yes, my friend, this country is sick...]

This passage speaks volumes about the linguistic
innovation characteristic of Lapiroisms. Lapiro's language
could be described as a melee of several codes. In his lyrics,

he tells the story of the disenchantment of the rank and file. To do so effectively, he is obligated to speak in a language that is intelligible to them. In 2001, Lapiro produced an album titled *Na You*, in which he took the ruling party (Cameroon People's Democratic Party—CPDM) to task for failing to halt the economic crisis and growing corruption plaguing the country. Another song, 'Constitution Constipée (Constipated Constitution) expresses Lapiro's strong objections to the constitutional amendment that has allowed President Paul Biya to stay in power after 2011. Both songs are sung in extremely veiled language. Lapiro uses language as an effective tool of communication. It is also a weapon of combat. He believes that music should be used as a strong tool to denounce oppression and power abuse. In his own words: "Music is a sort of weapon; sometimes instead of using guns, you use music, you use the voice, you use the sound and people who are against freedom will be shot down by your lyrics, by your sound, by your musical attitude"(Interview, 2010). *Mimba Wi, Lef am so, Small Mami, Pas argent pas amour, Ndinga Man Contre-attaque* are only a few of the many albums that have endeared Lapiro de Mbanga to many a Cameroonian music lover. Arguably the most talented Cameroonian musician, Lapiro is credited with having created the new slang called *Lapiroism*. He uses this language blend to mask the underlying messages in his songs. Lapiroism is undergirded by a phenomenon that Harvard Professor, Henri Louis Gates, Jr. equates with linguistic trickerism or signifying. Signifyin (g) is closely related to double-talk and trickery of the type used by monkeys, but, as Gates himself admits, "It is difficult to arrive at a consensus of definitions of signifying (261)." Bernard W. Bell defines this concept as an "elaborate, indirect form of goading or insult generally making use of profanity." Roger D. Abrahams writes that to signify is "to imply, goad, beg, and boast by indirect verbal or gestural means (260).

Conclusion

In sum, Lapiro de Mbanga is an anti-establishment songwriter who uses language judiciously to achieve his objective. He is both an entertainer and social critic. His danceable lyrics are both hosannas of hope and lamentations of the socially ostracized. He takes jibes at Cameroon's morally bankrupt leaders exemplified by dereliction of duty. His lyrics have an evocative appeal on an array of music connoisseurs on both sides of the Mungo River[17]. Lapiro's success in creating a novel slang bears testimony to the extraordinary talents of this self-taught musician. His songs have produced a tonic effect on a new breed of Cameroonian musicians who are primed to take over from their fallen icon. Committed musicians like Valsero and Elwood are already producing musical compositions that call into question impunity, administrative arrogance, bad governance, corruption, influence peddling and other social ills in Cameroon as the analysis in the following Chapter suggests.

---

[17] The Mungo River is a natural divide between the English-speaking and French-speaking Cameroons.

Chapter 5

Anti-establishment Lyrics of Lapiro, Valsero, and Elwood

The lyrics of Lapiro de Mbanga alias Ngata Man, Donny Elwood, and Valsero a.k.a 'Le Général' is telling. This trio has carved out a niche for themselves as valiant human rights activists in Cameroon. Their songs are lamentations for a native land in decrepitude.

The Lament of Elwood, Valerso and Lapiro

In a song titled 'Mon cousin militaire' [1], Donny Elwood deplores two cankers that have rendered the government of Cameroon dysfunctional, namely influence peddling and corruption. Listen to his lyrics:

Heureusement que/ j'ai mon cousin militaire,
Heureusement que/ j'ai mon cousin militaire,
Je serai déjà au cimetière,
Deux mettres sous terre,
Pauvre cadavre, simple squelette
En train de sourire comme
Tous les squelettes de la terre
Qui n'arrêtent pas de sourire,
Le sourire de la mort
Mort de misère,
Misère des hommes pauvres et macabres.
On m'appelle monsieur galère
On m'appelle tonton misère.
Je vis dans un quartier populaire,

Et nous sommes de vrais prolétaires,
Insuffisance alimentaire, vestimentaire, monétaire.
Et nous sommes de vrais prolétaires,
Nous sommes majoritaires sur cette terre de misère.
Heureusement que j'ai mon cousin militaire (…)
Quand il touche son salaire,
Il me donne mon argent de bière.
Et moi, je fonce chez ma rombière,
Toute la nuit on s'envole en l'air (…)
Quand il s'en va là-bas vers la guerre,
Moi, je fais des prières
Moi, je fais des patères austères.
Une mauvaise guerre,
Une guerre frontière,
Une guerre incendiaire,
Une guerre meurtrière,
Une guerre suicidaire (…)
[Thank Goodness I have a soldier cousin
Thank God I have a soldier cousin
I would be at the cemetery already
Two meters underground
Poor cadaver, simple skeleton
Smiling like all skeletons on this earth
Who never stop smiling
The smile of death
Death caused by misery
Misery that is the lot of the poor and the macabre
They call me Mr. Trouble
They call me Uncle Misery
I live in a ghetto
And we are real the proletariat
In need of food, clothes, and money
We are veritable proletariat

70

We are in the majority on this earth
Thank Goodness I have a soldier cousin (…)
When he earns his salary,
He gives me some money for beer.
I jump into my jalopy
And I roam the streets all night (...)
When he goes to war
I say my solemn prayers
A bad war,
A border war,
An inflammatory war,
A deadly war
A suicidal war (…)]

The lyrics of this song are pregnant with meaning. Elwood's reference to the Cameroonian military is significant. Under President Paul Biya, soldiers have become the most privileged group of people in Cameroonian society. Pampered with bloated salaries and perks, these partially educated servants of the state have nurtured an inordinate sense of their own grandeur. Rather than protect the citizenry, they have taken it upon themselves to brutalize and abuse their compatriots, especially in the event of public protests against the establishment, as was the case during the 2008 youth riots against the government for failing to put an end to skyrocketing gas and food prices.

Elwood bemoans the fate of the underprivileged of his land of birth: "The smile of death/ Death caused by misery/ Misery that is the lot of the poor and the macabre." The songwriter sings for the proletariat, the toiling masses who are subjected to brazen exploitation by the bourgeoisie of the corporate world — owners of means production. Elwood's song is the cry of a son of the soil whose heart throbs for his people, the majority of whom are living below poverty line, while a few people in government live in opulence. Like Fanon and Zola, Elwood, speaks for the downtrodden: the wretched of the earth of his society. He is the voice of voiceless Cameroonians. 'Mon cousin militaire' satirizes warmongering. I suppose that the war referenced in this song is the Nigeria-Cameroon conflict over the Bakassi Peninsula, a costly insane war that has no rationale at all.

In sum, Elwood uses his song as a medium through which he articulates his concerns over human rights abuses in his homeland. Language choice and diction pose no problem at all in this song. Unlike Lapiro de Mbanga, he writes his songs in simple intelligible French. The artist uses everyday French words and expressions known to the average Cameroonian. Colloquial terms like 'tonton' may elude the non-Cameroonian listener but context could be used to unravel the connotation of the word.

In another meaningful song titled 'En haut,' Elwood addresses the themes of influence peddling and corruption in Cameroon, as seen in the following excerpt:

Ma vie va changer
Le décret vient de tomber
Mon frère vient d'être nommé à un poste très élevé
La rumeur a circulé partout au quartier
Aujourd'hui, c'est confirmé.
La radio en a parlé, parlé, parlé.
La télé a confirmé (…)
Ça y est, ma vie va changer
Je vais enfin respirer
Je vais devoir me comporter
Comme un bao puisque mon frère est en haut.
La souffrance est terminée,

Terminée la marche à pied,
Les pains chargés,
Les taxis surchargés,
Ma vie va changer.
Je serai véhiculé,
J'irai partout dans les sous-quartiers
Me promener dans ma merco climatisée,
Toutes les filles vont tomber sans glisser (…)
Je vais gagner des marchés.
Mon frère est en haut.
Même si je ne peux pas livrer,
Il va quand même me payer.
Ma vie va changer.
Au village on va fêter,
On va bouger
On va boire
On va manger (…)
[My life will change
The decree has just landed
My brother has just been
 Appointed to a very high position
Rumor had circulated everywhere
In the neighborhood
Today it's a done deal
The radio had talked, talked, and talked
The TV has now confirmed it.
That's right, my life will change.
At last long, I will breathe.
I will behave like a Bao
Given that my brother is now
In a position of power
Gone are the days of hunger
Gone are the days of trekking

No more bread sandwiches
No more rides in overloaded taxis.
My life will change.
I shall possess a car
I will visit all the inner cities
In my air-conditioned Merco
All the girls will fall head
Over heels in love with me
I will be awarded contracts
My brother is highly placed
Even if I cannot deliver the services
For which I have been contracted
My brother will still pay me
My life will change
There will be feasting in the village,
People will come and go,
We will drink
We will eat (…)]

There is no gainsaying the fact that 'En haut' reads like a facsimile of Cameroon under Paul Biya. The cankers that Elwood lambastes in this musical tirade: abuse of power, influence peddling, corruption and nepotism are the common lot of Cameroonians living under this brutal dictator. The songwriter celebrates his brother's appointment to a top government position because he is certain that his brother will misuse his position to award him contracts even if he is unable to deliver the services for which he will be paid. Not only will he embezzle government money to buy expensive cars for his personal use but he will also use his position to abuse women: "Toutes les filles vont tomber sans glisser. This sort of unethical comportment on the part of civil servants is common currency in Cameroon under Paul Biya,

74

who himself is very corrupt and abuses power at will. He is commonly referred as the 'absentee landlord of Etoudi.' Biya spends nearly three-quarters of the year gallivanting in foreign lands in pursuit of nothing. This spells doom for the entire nation which is dire need of a clairvoyant leader.

As far as language is concerned, Elwood borrows extensively from Camfranglais[18] for the purpose of concealing certain significations from Cameroon's security forces as in the use of 'bao' for 'bigshot'. It should be noted that 'bao' is the abbreviated form of the word 'baobab.' In a similar vein, the word 'merco' is culled from Camfranglais. Camfranglophones use this word in reference to a posh car even if it is not of the Mercedez Benz brand. Elwood uses typical Cameroonianisms[19] in his songwriting in a bid to transpose the speech mannerisms of Cameroonian youths into the French language. Recourse to Camfranglais does not only taint Elwood's music with local color and flavor, but it also serves as an identity marker. Camfranglais is a slang meant to be understood only by initiated members of certain social groups: conmen, drug-peddlers, prostitutes, cabdrivers and more.

Elwood is not a lone voice in the vendetta against the cancerous society that Cameroon has become under Biya's regime. Valsero has followed in his footsteps. In a song titled 'Ce pays tue les jeunes' Valsero bemoans the fate of

---

[18] Camfranglais is a "composite language consciously developed by secondary school students who have in common a number of linguistic codes, namely French, English and a few widespread indigenous languages (Kouega, 2003: 23-29). Cameroonian youths use this urban slang as a communicative code to exclude other members of the community. They resort to Camfranglais to exchange ideas such as dating, sports, physical looks, and more in a manner that the message would remain coded.

[19] Cameroonian turns of phrase

Cameroon's lost generation — the young college and high school graduates whose future hangs in the balance on account of the Biya kleptocracy[20] headquartered in Yaounde:

Pour 2008 je me parle
Pour 2008 je te parle
J'espère que tu vas bien
Et qu'il t'arrivera des choses bien (…)
Tous ces diplômes chôment,
Cette génération ne verra pas le fameux bout du tunnel
De toutes les façons je n'y crois pas,
La jeunesse crève à petit feu,
Tandis que les vieux derrière les forteresses
Se saoulent à l'eau de feu
Ce pays tue les jeunes.
Cinquante ans de pouvoir
Après ça ils ne lâchent pas prise
De bled dénature (…)
La vie est trop dure
Le système la rend encore
Plus dure, plus dure,
Ils le vivent.
A Yaoundé ils le savent
Ce pays tue les jeunes.
Ce pays est comme une bombe
Pour les jeunes à tombeau.
Faites attention quand
Ça va péter ça va tuer
Tous les lambeaux
Alors les vieux, faites de la place.
Il faut pas le flambeau.

---

[20] Government by thieves

Ce pays tue les jeunes.
Les vieux ne lâchent pas la prise
De bled dénature (…)
[For the sake of 2008 I speak to myself
For 2008 I speak to you
I hope all is well with you
And I hope that good tidings will come your way (…)
All these graduates who are jobless
This generation that will never see
The proverbial light at the end of the tunnel
In any event, I don't believe they ever will
The youths are dying slowly
Whereas old folks are getting
Drunk in their bunkers
This county kills its youths
Fifty years in power
And yet they will not
Relinquish power peacefully
Life is too tough
The system makes it even tougher.
They experience it
In Yaounde, they know it.
This county kills its youths
This country is like a time-bomb
For the dying youths
Watch out! When it shall explode,
It shall destroy everyone
So, I am asking the older generation
To make way for the youths
Let's avoid flames
This county kills its youths.
The old folks will not relinquish power peacefully (…)]

Valsero's lyrics are fiery indeed. As I see it, his words are forebodings of tough times ahead. He is unapologetic in his opprobrium on a regime that destroys its own youths. In fact, this is the leitmotif in Valsero's song of protest. Notice the songwriter's deliberate repetition of the verse "Ce pays tue les jeunes." He does so in a bid to underscore the uncertain fate of youths in a country that has been governed by an unimaginative dictator for 30 years. As insinuated in the song, Paul Biya has transformed himself into a mother cow that feeds on its own offspring.

Valsero's reference to the year 2008 is significant given that this year constitutes an indelibly dark spot in Paul Biya's 30-year regime in Cameroon. Cameroonians remember that in February 2008 Biya ordered his blood-thirsty security forces to open fire on unarmed protesters, mostly youths, who had embarked on a protest match to vent their frustration against food and gas price hikes. The 2008 protests were a series of demonstrations in Cameroon's biggest cities like Yaounde, Douala, Buea and Bamenda. The government sent out troops to crack down on the unrest, and protesters were killed in hundreds. The government reported 40 people killed, but human rights groups claimed that the number was a lot higher. They also noted that more than 2,000 people were arrested in Douala alone and decried the trials as overly swift, secretive and severe.

It is interesting to note that Valsero perceives the macabre silence that hangs over the heads of Cameroonians as a time-bomb that will explode before long. He calls on the gang of kleptomaniacs hibernating in Yaounde to decamp before it is too late. Though singing in standard French, the singer infuses his lyrics with Cameroonianisms in order to be understood by the youths for whom he sings. Words like 'bled', 'crève' and 'se saoulent' [country, die and get drunk)] are colloquial French words chosen with circumspection by the songwriter to translate not only meanings but also emotions.

In 'Lettre au président' Valsero, a valiant freedom fighter, addresses his message directly to Paul Biya:

> Puis-je savoir, Prési,
> Pourquoi pour nous ça ne marche pas
> J'ai fait de longues années d'études
> Et j'ai pas trouvé d'emploi
> Je te rappelle que t'avais promis
> Qu'on sortirait du tunnel
> On y est toujours, ce sont les mêmes
> Qui tiennent la chandelle (…)
> Prési, tes potes vivent au bled
> Comme s'ils sont de passage
> Ils amassent des fortunes,
> Spécialistes des braquages
> Ils font preuve d'arrogance,
> Ils frustrent le peuple
> Ils piétinent les règles
> Et ils font ce qu'ils veulent
> Ah Prési, arrête ça c'est ça ton travail
> Ou inch'Allah, je jure, un autre fera le travail
> Le peuple n'en peut plus, les jeunes en ont marre
> On veut aussi goûter du miel sinon on te gare (…)
> Prési, les jeunes ne rêvent plus
> Prési, Prési, les jeunes n'en peuvent plus
> La majorité crève
> Dans le vice ils basculent
> Et quand le monde avance, nous, au
> Bled, on recule (…)
> Le peuple est souverain il n'a jamais tort,

Il a la force du nombre,
Il peut te donner tort
On n'a pas peur de la mort,
Même si tes potes appellent des
Flics en renfort
Ils disent de toi que c'est toi "l'homme lion"
Mais ils n'ont qu'un rêve: ils veulent tuer le lion.
[May I know, Presi, why nothing works for us
I have spent several years in school
But still can't find work
You must remember that you promised
Bringing us to the end of the tunnel
Here we are today still marking time,
While the same people call the shots (...)
Presi, your ministers live in this country
As if they were strangers on vacation
They amass wealth
They are schooled in the art of holdup
They are arrogant, and they frustrate the people
They flout laws, they act with impunity
Oh Presi, put an end to all this, that is your job
Otherwise, Insha'Allah, I swear
Someone else will do the job in lieu of you
The people cannot take it anymore
The youths are fed up
We want to have a taste of the honey too
Otherwise we will give you the boot (...)
Presi, the youths no longer have dreams
Presi, Presi, the youths cannot take it anymore
The majority of them are dying
They live in vice;
We retrogress in this country
While the rest of the world progresses

The people are sovereign, they are never wrong
They have the numerical strength
They can give you a vote of no-confidence
We are not afraid of death,
Even if your henchmen summon
Cops for protection
The people say you are the 'Lion Man']
But they dream of one thing only: kill the 'Lion.']

Valsero's interrogative missive to Paul Biya is incisive.
Not only does he take the president to task for promises not
kept, he also enjoins him to perform the job for which his is
paid. The song is an acrimonious diatribe that conveys the
anger of the Cameroonian people frustrated with a regime
that has failed them in every aspect. The sagacious rapper
demands responses from Biya on a number of thorny issues,
not least of which is the reason for governmental
malfunction. He revisits the vexing theme of chronic
employment in Cameroon and the predicament of college
graduates who cannot find gainful employment.

In a nutshell, 'Lettre au président' is the cry of a
disenchanted Cameroonian at odds with a regime that excels
in arrogance, insolence, double-speak impunity, and
dereliction of duty. Valsero deems it fit to inform the
president that the Cameroonian people have defeated fear
and that one day, God willing, someone else will do the job
he is unable to do to the satisfaction of the Cameroonian
electorate. This apocalyptic admonishment ought to be taken
seriously by the powers-that-be.

Linguistically speaking, this song is more colloquial than
'Ce pays tue les jeunes.' The reason is that Valsero is speaking
on behalf of the Cameroonian youths and has chosen to
employ a parlance that is characteristic of the social class for

whom he is spokesperson. The musician constantly culls words and expressions from Camfranglais as seen in the following examples: 'tiennent la chandelle' (perform a duty), 'en ont marre' (fed up), 'bled' (home, country, and village), 'potes' (friends, henchmen, comrades), and 'crèvent' (die). These words fit into the register of 'youth talk' in Cameroon. It is interesting to note that Valsero transposes foreign language words into French. The Arabic word 'Insha'Allah' is an example of such loans. Listeners who may be familiar with the linguistic plurality in Cameroon would not be surprised. Cameroon is a multilingual country with over 248 indigenous languages. Musicians constantly borrow from these native tongues as has been discussed above. Valsero has recourse to an expression to which all Cameroonians have been accustomed: 'L'homme lion 'or 'Lion man,' has become a sobriquet for Paul Biya on account of the brutality with which he responds to legitimate complaints from citizens about governmental ineptitude. Valsero is believed to have copied this style of songwriting from his mentor, Lapiro de Mbanga.

Lapiro is the only musician in the trio that has borne the brunt of Paul Biya's offhanded reaction to political dissidence. In a song titled 'Lef am so,' he bemoans the fate of his native land as follows:

Mola, taim weh person get daso one sick
For yi sikin yi get espoir sei da sick fit bolè
But taim weh sick beaucoup
Like how di kondre get'am so
Surtout how weh kan kan traitement à perfusions
Ana traitement de choc noba bolè yi,
Je jure que yi own mandat done shot.
All we we sabi sei taim weh sick noba bolè for l'hôpital
Dem di replier na for kanda sitik

Comment se fait-il que plus we win back
Plus kondre di so so meng daso?
Mombo, avant foua no be been
Jess noh, na manguru ngwet don been
Pourtant banque mondiale ana a la instituts financiers
Dem don trust we ndoh avec majorations de crédit
Remboursable dans cent ans (...)
Dat be sei sep njaka for njaka for we njaka
Dem go come boulot for pay dang ndoh.
Donc, non seuelment we sep we don ton na ninga
We don bata hypothéquer avenir for we njaka forever and
ever (...)
Ignorance avec mépris
Arrogance et insolence for dem kondre pipo (...)
Comme vous pouvez le constater,
Cameroon dong capside...
Yes, mombo, this country no well (...)
[If you are afflicted with only one disease,
There may be some hope of recovery
But if you are down with
Several illnesses like this country of ours
And all kinds of treatment, including drips
And anti-shock medication have not helped
I swear, you can be sure your days are numbered
We all know that when hospital medications fail us
We fall back on traditional medicine as an alternative
How can you explain the fact that the more medications
we
Give to our nation, the worse its health becomes?
My friend, in the past there was no poverty in this
country
Today, people are merely scraping a bare living

Yet the World Bank and other international financial institutions
  Have loaned us money with incredibly high interest rates
  Payable in one hundred years
  In other words, our great grandchildren
  Shall have to work in order to repay these loans
  So, we have not only been reduced to slaves
  We have also mortgaged the future of our kids forever and ever (...)
  Ignorance and spitefulness
  Arrogance and insolence in dealing with compatriots
  As you can see for yourselves
  This country is topsy turvy
  Cameroon has capsized
  Yes, my friend, this country is sick indeed.]

This song speaks volumes about the despondency the songwriter harbors in his heart. He argues in his song that Cameroon is a sick nation hunkered down by huge loans obtained from Breton Woods institutions, notably the World Bank: "Pourtant banque mondiale ana ala instituts financiers/Dem don trust we ndoh avec majorations de credit." This song touches on the problem of debt servicing in Cameroon and Africa at large. Lapiro insinuates that external loans are the cancer of Africa. He contends that until Cameroon gets rid of foreign debts, citizens will continue to live in abject poverty. The linguistic innovation characteristic of Lapiro's musical composition has been discussed at length in previous chapters. Suffice it to say that language is a very powerful tool in the hands of Lapiro de Mbanga. His language is in synchrony with the messages proffered.

Conclusion

In a nutshell, Lapiro, Elwood, and Valsero tower over their peers in very many respects—unparalleled creative acumen, mental agility, keen attention to detail, and enviable in vocal skills. They are fervent believers in social justice.

Their anti-establishment songs bear testimony to the stuff of which they are made. They are both entertainers and social critics. Their danceable lyrics translate messages of hope for better days in Cameroon. The theme that runs through the songs of all three musical combatants is empowerment of the socially ostracized. Their songs have produced a powerful effect on the new generation of young Cameroonians who are prepared to take the future of their country into their own hands. Awilo is one such upcoming musician. Language is a mighty tool at the disposal of these songwriters. They wield it tactfully. While Elwood has kept his French in a pristine standard form, Valsero and Lapiro have gone with the flow and created an urban slang that not only reflects the speech mannerisms of Cameroonian youths but also harbors revolutionary ideas. The musical stuff produced by Lapiro, Valsero and Elwood provide excellent material for creative writing. In the following chapter, we will dwell on some fictional works written in honor of Lapiro de Mbanga.

Chapter 6

Fictionalizing the Rebel Art of Lapiro de Mbanga

Ndinga Man
Lapiro de Mbanga alias Ndinga Man,
Né Pierre-Roger Sandjo à Mbanga,
Lapiro, musicien chevronné, ne bi so ?
Ouais ! Ouais! Lapiro,
Ndinga Man Numéro Un,
C'est comme ça, no ?
Yes ! Yes!
Tara no make erreur!
Lapiro de Mbanga a.k.a Ngata Man,
Trouble-fête national, ne bi so?
Lapiro, véritable small no bi sick,
Enfant terrible de la maison, no be so?
Yes ! Yes! En avant Tara!
Go before, go before Tara!
We day for youa back Tara!
Motion! Motion de soutien!
Lapiro, djintete Ndinga Man
Wei yi dei Mbanga, no be so?
Ouais! Ouais!
Yi own musique na musique
Pour les damnés de la terre, n'est-ce pas?
Yes! Yes!
Lapiro, président des sauveteurs, no be so?
Ouais! Ouais!
Lapiro, porte-parole des sans voix, no be so?
Yi own musique na musique for
Les laissés-pour-compte, non?

Biensûr! Biensûr!
Lapiro de Mbanga, bao ongolais, no bi so?
Bête noire des fossoyeurs de la
République bananière, no be so?
Ouais! Ouais!
Lapiro, moustique politique,
C'est comme ça, non? Yes! Yes!
Lapiro, la voix des voix silencieuses, no be so?
Biensûr! Biensûr!
Yi own musiki na for
Put shame fot djintete
Long crayon dem head, no be so?
Ouais! Ouaisi!
Lapiro, bête noire insupportable, n'est-ce pas?
Killjoy des chope-broke- pots, no be so? Yes! Yes!
Lapiroisme, Hymne des déshérités, no be so?
Ouais! Ouais!
Lapiroisme, Appel de clairon
Pour la révolution prolétaire, no be so?
Biensûr! Biensûr!
Lapiroisme, chant de libération
C'est comme ça, non?
Yes! Yes!
Lapiroisme, hymne de dissidence, no be so?
Ouais! Ouais!
Lapiroisme, hymne funèbre des orphelins, no be so?
Yes! Yes! Gee me chance make I shake ma skin,
Makossa dei me for foot!
Dégagez! Dégagez!
J'ai envie de danser le makossa.
Gee me road make
I shake ma kongolibon head!
Makossa dei me for head!

88

Mouf me de make I shake ma waist,
Makossa dei me for lass!
Put me dong make I shake ma banja,
Makossa dei me side by side!
Bukulu! Bukulu! Saka! Saka!
Dansez! Dansez! Ku yi rawa!
Lapiro, CPDM pet peeve, oye!
Lapiro, Mbiya's nightmare, oye!
Lapiro de Mbanga, tête brulée, oye!
Lapiro Ndinga Man, oye!
Lapiro! Albatros de Popol, oye!
Lapiro Ngata Man, oye!
Lapiro héros national, oye!
Lapiro, l'homme qui n'est plus
Mais qui vit à jamais, no be si?
Yes! Yes!
Lapiro, fallen national hero, oye!
Lapiro, the man that refuses to die, oye!
Lapiro, the people's idol, abi na so no?
Yes! Yes!

Cameroon Na Cameroon

Ma complice dem for Nkouloulou-o!
Ma tara dem for Moloko-o!
Ma mombo dem for Marché central-o!
Ma kombi dem for Kumba market-o!
Ma dong pipo dem for Kasala farm-o!
Di wan dem for Camp Sic de Yabassi-o!
Ma complice dem for prison de Tchollire-o!
Di wan dem for 'Maximum security
Prison' for Mantoum-o!
Sef da wan dem for Kondengui.
I say mek I langua wuna dis tori.

Some hymne national dong commot
Just now for Ongola.
Da mean say some national anthem
Dung show head for we own kontri.
Da anthem dem di sing'am say:
Le Cameroun c'est le Cameroun,
Da mean say,
Cameroon is Cameroon, alors.
In ala word,
Cameroon na Cameroon, ah ha!

You wan pass for any corner,
You di daso ya say,
Le Cameroun c'est le Cameroun,
On va faire comment, alors?
Da mean say,
Cameroon is Cameroon;
We go na how-no?
Na so dat we own Cameroon National Anthem day!

Grand Katika for Ngola tif all doh
Go put'am for bank for Mbeng,
We di daso cry say,
Cameroon na Cameroon,
We fit do na wheti sef, no?
Na so da we own Cameroon National Anthem day!

Koukouma mof all nchou
For yi office go put'am
For banda for yi long,
Antoine Ntsimi, alias Ali Baba,
We di daso sing say: merde alors!
Après tout, le Cameroun c'est le Cameroun,

Tu as déjà vu quoi?
Da mean say:
You dong nye wheti sef?

Katika for CRTV
Bring yi kontri pipo come fullup
Office dem day,
We go daso sing say,
Cameroon na Cameroon,
Massa, wheti we fit do sef no?
Na so da Cameroon National Anthem day!

Mange mille katch taximan
For road take all yi moni,
We go daso kop nye,
We di daso sing say,
Bo, garri dung pass wata-o!
Wheti we fit do no?
No bi na Cameroon dis?
Na so da Cameroon National Anthem day!

Docta nyoxer sick woman
For inside hospita, we daso tok say:
It never rains but it pours!
Da woman yi massa go daso tok say,
Ma broda, na dem get kontri,
You wan mek I do na how?
Cameroon na Cameroon.
Na so da Cameroon National Anthem day!

Gomna deny for put coal tar
For Bamenda road bekoz
SDF dei for dei,

Pipo go daso shake head,
Dem tok say, cheh!
Kontri man, we go do na how no?
Cameroon na Cameroon.
Na so da Cameroon National Anthem day!
Dem compresser wok pipo
For Cameroon Marketing Board,
For CDC, or for Socapalm
Dem go daso wrap dem tail
for dem lass like tif dog,
Tok say: Papa God we go do na how-eh?
Cameroon na Cameroon.
Na so da Cameroon National Anthem day!

Pikin commot for sarako,
Yi no get boulot,
Yi papa wit yi mami
Go daso put dem hand for dem head,
Dem tok say: yeh maleh!
You must go drive bendskin,
We go do na how?
Cameroon is Cameroon.
Na so da Cameroon National Anthem day!
Grand Kamambrou for Ngola constipé constitution
Bekoz yi wan die for Etoudi,
Camers dem go daso tok say,
Wandas shall never end in Ngola!
Frères on va faire comment alors?
Est-ce que les gens
De Bamenda vont accepter ça?
Le Cameroon c'est le Cameroun, no?
Na so da Cameroon National Anthem day!

Mbere-khaki shoot bendskineur kill'am
Bekoz yi dong deny for tchoko,
Ala bendskinneur dem go daso,
Pick Tokyo go for inside matango club,
Begin souler di cry say
Weh, massa! Mon vieux,
Le dehors est mauvais,
On va faire même comment?
Le Cameroon c'est le Cameroun.
Na so da Cameroon National Anthem day!

Chop Pipo Dem Moni party
Truqué élection à vue d'oeil,
Ongolais dem go daso bend head
For grong dem cry say:
Wuyo! Wuyo! Na how we go do-eh?
Cameroon na Cameroon, true true.
Na so da Cameroon National Anthem day!

Grand katika,
Tif moni go tie hospita
For Baden-Baden for mukala kontri,
Camers dem go daso knack hand, jua jua!
Dem cry say: vrai de Dieu!
Some wan dem di toli say:
Mon Dieu! Ne criez pas trop fort!
Le Cameroun c'est le Cameroun
Na so da Cameroon National Anthem day!

Le Père de la Nation,
Ancient chaud gars,
Da mean say Father of the Nation,
Old hot dude,

Go carry ashawo come put'am
For palais de l'unité,
Say na First Lady,
Ongalais dem go soso knack mop say:
Dan sapak dem upside kain kain-o!
Vraiment le Cameroun est cauchemardesque,
Vivons seulement.
Da mean say,
Cameroon na lass,
Impossible n'est pas camerounais!
Mek we begin nye daso.
C'est le comble!
Cameroon na Cameroon
So no, dis palava dont pass
Some kokobioko professor for Ongola,
Yi shake yi head two time,
Yi say: this country blows my mind!
"This is the last straw
That broke the camel's back,
Cameroon is Cameroon"
Na so da Cameroon National Anthem day!

Ngomna for Renouveau
Na tif pipo beaucoup!
Dem cut pipo dem salaires
Sef ten taim for one year,
Ma kontri pipo dem go daso
Run go for mimbo hose,
Begin knack njakiri say:

Massa, I never see dis kain
Wan before. Yi dung pass ma sense.
Na which kain barlok dis-no?

Cameroon na Cameroon.
Na so da Cameroon National Anthem day!
Clando ngomna tcha Lapiro de Mbanga
Go put'am for ngata,
Mek yi ton prisoner without no crime!
All ninga pipo dem for Ngola
Dem go daso tok sa: çaaaa!!
On n'a jamais vu ça!
Mais on va faire alors comment?
No be Cameroon na Cameroon?

Yeye Katika for Ngola
Katch Joe la Conscience,
Alias Kameni Joe de Vinci
Go lock'am for Kondengui,
After dem send milito dem go meng
Yi pikin called Aya Kameni Patrick Lionel,
All 'freedom fighter' dem for Cameroon,
Dem go soso bend head for dem armpit,
Dem tok side: upside dong keleng keleng,
Any man fain yi long
Cameroon na Cameroon!

I dong ya dis allo anthem sotai,
I shake ma head.
I check for ma head sei,
Dis Cameroon wey dem di tok so,
Yi dei daso for dis grong,
Or na for ala planet?
I di wanda!
Je wanda seulement
Parce que ce que nous vivons
Dans ce pays, hmmmm!

Na Bob Marley bi sing yi own anthem say:
"Liberate yourselves from mental slavery!"
I gring gi'am for Bob
Forseka say ongolais dem be vrais ningas
C'est à dire, mbutuku Slave Number One!

Hommage à un Combattant qui n'est plus
Ancien chaud gars na mouilleur!
Step down! Démissionnez!
Because you dong over massacré constitution...
You dong over échouer
Subordination du pouvoir judiciaire na you!

Subordination du pouvoir législatif na you!
Manoeuvre politique avec impunité na soso you!
Step down! Démissionnez!
Because you dong over mouiller!
Insécurité généralisée—
Chavoum dong hala for banque for Bonaberi
Fusils dong hala for Pont de Wouri
Dem dong meng your chef de terre,
Kamambrou for Bakassi
You dong over mouiller!

Step down! Démissionnez!
Ngueme and chômage
Dong multiplié for dis mboko
Bendskinneurs, chauffeurs clandos,
Laveurs de voitures, tackleurs, sauveteurs

Bayam sellams, coiffeurs and coiffeuses ambulantes
For marché central, call-boxeurs and call-boxeuses
Dem di pointer na for dong rain and for dong sun

96

Preuve, dem di kick muna bébés
For maternité everywhere for we own kondre.

No be youa boulot na sécurisation
Des personnes et de leurs biens?
A vrai dire this one na échec total
If you no fit garantir sécurité sep for nourrissons!
Step down! Démissionnez! You dong over mouiller!

Ndamba
Koukouma, you must sabi
Say dis youa own équipe Lions Domptables
Que vous avez formée c'est seulement le sissia.
Vous avez trop échoué,
Défaite sur défaite, comment!

Kamambrou,
Il faut know que ndamba na sense
Ndamba ce n'est pas le boum boum!
If your joueurs them di mouiller
It's your faut car c'est vous le coach.

Koukouma,
Pour marquer les buts
Il faut éviter le boum boum!
Mola, ndamba na sense
Ndamba no be tchouquer tchouquer.

Coach, vous avez trop échoué,
You must give chance
For ala man better than you are
Ancien chaud gars,
Your mandat don bolè.

Youa Lions Domptables
Na distributeurs de points
Vos joueurs sont les loss-sense.
You must démissionner! Step down!
Like youa répé way been dash you chia!

Démissionnez! Step down!
Parce que vos joueurs
Ne font que ndima ndima
Ils ne font que njoum njoum! Step down!
Si non le peuple vous demandera leur compte!

Je Wanda Avec Lapiro
Il y a quelque chose que
Je wanda depuis from,
If par hazard, I say par hasard
Because le locataire d'Etoudi
Ne croit aucunément in the truth of this dictum:
"From dust you came, and to dust you shall return."

Anyhow, si le mandat de Paul Biya parvient à bolè today
That be say, il crève bon gré mal gré,
Who will take his place as père de la nation?
Je wanda seulement et je sabi que
Beaucoup de camers wanda comme moi.
Est-que je dis vrai ou non?

Don't forget that la relève ne
Se prépare pas au Cameroun, hein.
Si Biya crève today, certainement que
Son mandat va bolè un jour, fais quoi fais quoi,
Est-ce que na that garçon de courses
Que vous appelez Cavayé Yéguié Djibril,

Rejeton des parents kirdi from Mada
In the Mayo Sara arrondissement,
Na yi go chop chia ou alors
C'est le soi-disant président du Sénat fantôme
That does not exist qui va squatter à Etoudi
Until further notice, Je wanda seulement?

De toutes les façons, we no wan
Nye zangalewa for Etoudi si
Popol parvient à crever for better or for worse!
 L'Ongola mérite mieux que les zangalewa half-book
Dem go come nous foutre le bordel
Partout dans le bled.
Nous wandarons seulement.

Lapiro, Apprenti-Sorcier
Dommage à tous ces bouc-émissaires!
Dommage surtout à Hamidou Marafa,
Ce Bao qui est fall du pouvoir
Quand ce djimtété est come au pouvoir depuis from
On lui avait tok que lookot Popol,

Because quand vous n'êtes plus
Dans les good books de l'Homme Lion,
Il risque de vous foutre that coup de tête
Qu'il avait sissia to Eric Chinje.
Lors de l'interview infâme.

But Marafa avait refusé carrément de nous ya.
Il nous avait seulement answer que:
Capos, that wuna own langua na daso allô.
Alors, le voilà aujourd'hui dans la taule inside Kondengui.
Every day, il ne cesse de crier, wohoo! Wohoo!

Popo me I di askam say hein,
Wusai ndiba go commot for come move
Hamido Marafa for that Kondengui fire?
Mbombo, tell me: Qui a raison?
Just now qui est le vrai mboutman?

Est-c'est nous ou c'est Hamido Marafa?
A vous de juger!
Some Aboki don nyè dis palava,
Sotai il a dit seuelment que
A malin malin et demi!

Chiba D'après Lapiro
J'accuse les politiquarts cameriens
D'être non seulement mboutoucous
But en même temps des feymans.
Je les accuse tous—opposants et Rdépécistes
Because ils ne font que pratiquer la belly politics.

J'accuse les tontons macoutes ongolais
Etant donné que dem don ton be na
Les vampires de la République.
Mola, langua-moi!
Comment toi-même tu nyè cette aff, no?

Est-ce ma tchat c'est seulement le sissia?
Whether na Paul Biya
Or c'est Ni John Fru Ndi, ou Ndam Njoya,
N'est-ce pas eux tous, ils mangent le même soya?
How you check say dem fit tok true tok?

Vraiment, où est la différence,
Que ce soit Popol ou l'originaire de Ntarikon à Etoudi,

N'est-ce pas dem all na kick pipo?
Na wa for dis we own kondre-o!
Nos politiquarts nous font voir kan-kan wahala.

J'accuse les politiquarts ongolais
Because ils sont tous les kickmans,
Transformés en élus du peuple.
Je veux qu'on les foute tous en taule
Yes mbombo, dat be say dem must yua ngata!

We don tok! One day one day
Ali Baba et ses quarante voleurs
Must yua ngata, sans oublier le bao locataire
Du quat du peuple à Etoudi
Because Popol sep sep na popo Kengué.

Plaidoyer De Lapiro De Mbanga
 Grand Camarade, El Hajj
Je check say nous tous on le know.
Ce dictateur qui avait foutu le Cameroun
En l'air avant de donner
Son chia à son nchinda—ancien chaud gars.
Ce bandit beti qui plume le Cameroun à vue d'oeil.

Il est bien vrai que les politiquarts
Sont one and the same partout sur notre planète.
C'est même pour cela que je wanda
Au sujet des dépouilles du Grand Camarade,
Abandonnées à Dakar depuis from.
Why must Ahijdo's remains stay in Dakar?

Je wanda surtout why Popol
N'a pas utilisé son number six pour

Fait venir la carcasse de ce pauvre
Musulman whey yi been dash yi chia.
Pourquoi ne pas ramener ses dépouilles
Ne serait-ce que pour calmer les esprits troublés?

Il y a des taras qui nous remplissent
Les oreilles avec leur brouhaha choir
Selon lequel Grand Camarade fut
Un meilleur kamambrou que Popol
Je leur tok carrément de shut up,
Parce qu'ils ne savent rien de ce qu'ils langua.

Ces mbombos n'ont qu'à aller tchatcher avec
Les baos comme Reuben Um Nyobé,
Ernest Ouandié, Félix Moumié, Albert Ndongmo,
Albert Womah Mukong et Wambo le Courant,
And then dem go sabi pourquoi je check say
Grand Camarade était un diable comme les autres.

Au vu de ces choses
Faudrait-il peut-être langua que
Un bon politiquart na daso
De one way yi don meng,
Autrement dit, il faut être cadavéré
Pour être un bon politiquart.

Mola, how you sep you nyè dis palava no?
Les camers plenty ont tchatté à Mbiya que,
Non, non et non, vous ne pouvez pas
Abandonner l'ancien kamambrou là
Dans une piètre sépulture dans un quat étranger.
Soyons sérieux! 6 avril ou non.
Même so, Popo reste impertubable

Hanté comme il est
By the ghost of Grand Camarade.
Il ne veut carrément ya nothing
A propos de cette affaire vachement politisée.
Les appels sont tombés sur les deaf ears!
Dommage au Grand Camarade
Qui n'a jamais pas pris le temps de bien connaître
Le mec Beti à qui il avait largué son chia,
Ce scélérat connu sous le nom de Paul Biya.
Je dirais donc au Grand Camarade, Achouka !

Coup De Fil De Lapiro A Ni John Fru Ndi
I say hein, wuoh!
Quand on est vieux,
On est vieux no be so?
Le pouvoir appartient
A ceux qui se lèvent tôt.
Laissez-moi tchatcher la vérité à Fru Ndi.

If you want say make some man
Gee chance for road, you sep must
Learn for gee chance for road
For some other mola
Wey yi dey for youa back.

The truth of the matter be say,
Charity begins at home.
We be di check say sometime
Chairman go gee chance for some jeune talent
Make yi corriger Pa Pol.

But sep so, Pa for Ntarikon say
Ngumba must cry for Etoudi,

Yi say Ngumba close must enter Palais.
Ah ah, Je wanda que depuis 1990
This vieux capable dong be katika
For SDF jusqu'ai ce jour!

Time waits for nobody
If we want make some man gee
Chance for road, we sep must
Learn for gee chance for ala man
Way yi day for we back.

Ce que dirait Lapiro à First Lady
Chantal Pulchérie Vigouroux Biya,
La belle de la République
Ou mami wata qui bouffe
Les mbourous de notre cher pays?

This nkane elle est même quoi?
La mami wata de la République
Ou bien notre première dame?
Je wanda seulement-o
Because si vraiment elle est notre first lady

Pourquoi alors elle sape
Comme une vraie wolowoss?
Est-ce seulement pour attirer
Les yos et les jeunes talents
Etant donné que son ancien chaud gars

Is no longer très chaud?
Ekié! Je wanda only.
Ou alors c'est pour show off tout court
Comme c'est le petit modèle des metoches?

Nous voulons sabi quand même.

Chantal Pulchérie Vigouroux Biya,
Avec le nkap du peuple camerounais
Qu'elle a kick de la caisse noire d'Etoudi,
Elle est devenue mami wata, mini minor
On top of being notre première dame!

C'est Popol qui a cherché
And he dong trouva
Just now he must supporta
And for dat supporta
Il faut se méfier car la femme qui a connu la rue, ssshhh!

The passing of Lapiro de Mbanga has triggered a volley of praises and eulogies from friends at home and in the diaspora. The following chapter is a compendium of elegies and lamentations for the fallen hero.

Chapter 7

Eulogies and Obituaries for the fallen Hero

The first of these panegyrics is Herbert Boh's stellar write-up captioned "My Tribute to Cameroon's Best Political Activist Ever" published in the *AFOaKOM* forum:

My Tribute to Cameroon's Best Political Activist Ever By Boh Herbert.

It was a Sunday in the early 1990s. It was one of only two days every week for six months when Cameroon pretended to be a normal country. Citizens did brisk business on Saturday and Sunday. Monday through Friday, Cameroon sank into the civil disobedience campaign code-named "ghost town." Excluding the pre- and post-independence armed struggle, this was unprecedented political revolt for a country that advertises the docile nature of its citizens as proof it is an island of peace.

In a small hall on a campus owned by the Presbyterian Church in Bamenda, about three dozen leaders of political dissidents—the coalition later named the Union for Change—the group that had engineered the revolt, were gathered to take stock, refine strategies as they did frequently... switching towns each time.

The firebrand leader of the Students' Parliament reiterated the commitment of students to bring about the country of their dreams, decrying "the monster at Etoudi" who he said was preventing that dream from becoming reality. A Douala-based lawyer laid out what the law provides and what it forbids, cautioning the leaders gathered to seek a cunning path by finding and taking the many legal cracks on the books. Another Douala-based computer expert spoke of how the cause could win support from the West now that it had mobilized the people, and of the promise that new information technology held for helping spread liberty and transform countries across Africa.

Then a musician spotting smart low-heel white relax shoes, a pair of wrangler jeans, a white T-shirt and a sleeveless jeans jacket rose to speak. You could hear a pin drop as Sandjo Lambo Pierre Roger (Lapiro) prepared to speak. Also known affectionately by millions of his fans as "Ndinga Man" for his immense talent as a guitarist, Lapiro died last March 16 in Buffalo, New York. He was 56.

While it can be said that the "ghost towns" were begotten, not made by yet another hero from the grassroots, Mboua Massock, it was Lapiro de Mbanga who became its undisputed spiritual leader and community organizer. At that Presbyterian Church Center meeting, hosted by the then relatively unknown and timid-to-a-fault SDF leader, Ni John Fru Ndi, it was Lapiro who played king and/or king- maker. It was clear to everyone at this meeting or others before and after it, that Lapiro was way up in the pecking order within the fast-growing squadron of opposition leaders. Speaking in that trade mark mixture of French, English and Pidgin "Made in Ndinga Man's Head," he called for unity among leaders who must, he stressed, remember to serve the people –the poor –"et non se server"… as they work to initiate swift, decisive action needed to oust the dictatorship in the capital, Yaounde. "Na Etoudi be we destination," he said in that impeccable Franglais he coined.

I had known Lapiro, the musician. Just a few months earlier, I believe, I had taken my spouse – at the time my fiancée – to a music concert at Cinema Abbia, where Makossa legend Ben Decca was scheduled to play for the very last time on one of those his many, many retirement concerts that were always followed by a comeback and then another retirement gig. It was a Ben Decca event, so to speak, but the only reason we (my spouse and I) had gone was to see Lapiro bring down the house.

At Cinema Abbia that night, it was Lapiro, the musician and Boh Herbert, one of Lapiro's fans. At the Presbyterian Church Center, Boh Herbert the journalist was still adjusting to Lapiro, the very savvy political animal. In a career that saw him rub shoulders with musical immortals and saints like Jimmy Cliff and Fela Ransom Kuti, Lapiro used his art as a weapon to win freedom, foster democracy, denounce abuse, advance the cause of the poor, decry injustice, lend his voice to the voiceless and defy the tyrant in power to resign or be forced, by the will of the people, to accept an overdue change of guard at the helm of state.

Events in 1991, notably the mistake the regime made to arrest Celestin Monga and Pius Njawe following Monga's Open Letter in *Le Messager*, proved that Lapiro had an unnerving ability not only to hit the right musical notes, but also to hit the right chord, right at the heart of the political system. I remember, as a BBC correspondent, how my headquarters at Bush House London was confused about whether I should stay in the courthouse and follow proceedings in the case or stick outside the courtroom, where Lapiro and tens of thousands of his fans held their own court to decry the Kangaroo court the regime had in place. He led the army of pro-democracy activists not by ordering foot soldiers to do his bidding, but by marching ahead into battle and seeking approval from his followers in political protests as in real life with the wordings: "Mokolo, Ah Chakara?"

The Monga-Njawe trial served in many ways as a spark, awakening Lapiro the musician, human rights activist, freedom fighter and politician. Yaounde found out later to its chagrin that the combustible mix of protest rap, rhumba and 'kill-man-pay' "Soukouss Boogie" that Lapiro had long proved he had for dancers and music lovers also had enough fire to bring down dictatorship.

As a "soldat de première heure," Lapiro understood better than most the true nature of some of the opposition leaders Cameroonians had trusted with their aspirations. That is why once some "ghost town" operations turned violent, notably in Douala, and an underground business selling the famous "carton rouge à Paul Biya," extorting funds from some and abusing certain youngsters, Lapiro took the risks to speak up. Today, a majority of those who thought he crossed the carpet into the ruling CPDM by speaking out on state television feel guilt and even a certain sense of remorse for ignoring the telltale signs of the power hungry opposition. Lapiro's prophecy that the opposition, as structured or not structured was a bunch of "Big Mop for Nothing" has come true. Many, if not all the opposition leaders that Lapiro denounced as seeking power for the sake of it have long proven, indeed, that they seek only an open-ended contract to lead their parties "until death do them part."

Lapiro's biggest error in that whole saga in which he was accused by his fans of "chopping soya," and going to the extent of trying to lynch him in Douala and, in the process smashing windows on the glass building of the SITABAC building where he had to take refuge... his main error, I believe, was that Lapiro trusted State television to show the entire statement he had made. Instead, State television edited out all the parts of the declaration in which Lapiro lambasted the regime in power and broadcast only those parts of it in which he was calling his peers in the opposition to order. In hindsight, it is clear that the songwriter and singer of "No

Make Erreur" did not heed his own advice and opponents within the regime and the opposition shamelessly capitalized on it to try to discredit him.

Lapiro was forced thereafter to frequently explain what truly happened, including in songs like "Na Wou Go Pay." He fought to re-establish his honor and to undo a smear campaign of outrageous proportions that the regime in Yaounde skillfully rolled out against him, relying on the dreaded leader of the secret police, the late Jean Fochive, and an unscrupulous, outright dirty "do me, ah do you" opposition.

A book that Lapiro had completed but has died before publishing will clear the clouds of the deceit that surrounded these events. Shortly after moving to the USA in 2012, Lapiro and I exchanged several emails discussing the translation of the book into English. I committed in life to him that I will handle the translation. That promise is one I cannot wait to be given the honor to fulfill. The book, he had suggested to me, explains many unsolved mysteries and contains many a revelation. In closing, let me confess that I hate to break bad news... I have to, thought... so, here it is.

It is no longer a secret, after Lapiro that the government of Cameroon has specialized in administering death to its most formidable political opponents and dissidents, using prison as the slaughter house or as the transit station "en route" to the grave. We also now know that denying medical care to prisoners is not just negligence. It is part of an assassination plot, meticulously executed.

After decades of never-ending police harassment, including sabotage of his means of livelihood such as the burning down of his nightclub in Mbanga... after three years in prison on charges that masked the real reason for his condemnation—which was his courageous campaign in

February 2008 to decry the extension of the presidential terms under a "Constitution Constipée" that sadly institutionalized an empire in Cameroon... After calling out for "Envoyer tout le monde à Kondengui," it is instead "Ngata Man," as Lapiro renamed himself after his time in the big house... that, even in death, is having the last laugh, by denying the regime in Yaounde the never-ending affixing of medals of honor on those it kills.

Sadly for regime in Yaounde and happily for all of us... happily for Lapiro's family, his friends, and his fans... it just so happens that when you are chief, as Lapiro was chief for his people of Mbanga, death has no power over you. As our people say the chief has "disappeared." Lapiro is missing! Our tradition demands that we find him. So, let me offer these words of condolence to all who mourn him: Long live Lapiro de Mbanga! Long live Lapiro de Buffalo, New York!

Patrice Nganang's masterful piece titled "Le règne du faux maquis: à propos de Lapiro et Ateba Eyene" published in the *Cameroon Politics* social forum is breath-taking:

Le Rène Du Faux Maquis: A Propos De Lapiro Et Ateba Eyene, Patrice Nganang.

Je suis à Yaoundé et je vois la même chose. Eh oui, il parait que ces 28 et 29 mars, les restes de Lapiro de Mbanga sont (aussi) en train d'être remis aux cieux quelque part. Dans la tyrannie la plus vieille d'Afrique, le Cameroun, 'le peuple,' on nous dira, 'spontanément s'est choisi un héro national', et c'est Charles Ateba Eyene celui-là. Aux dernières nouvelles dans ce pays nommé Cameroun, Lapiro faisait plutôt la une des journaux qui l'accusaient d'avoir couché avec sa propre fille mineure, ces journaux l'accusaient d'avoir, je ne sais plus trop fait quoi, Lapiro qui, avait pourtant passé toutes les instances juridiques de la terre qui avaient déclaré son incarcération sans objet. Excellente que cette vie sienne qui était calquée sur celle de Fela à qui à sa mort des funérailles nationales avaient été données au Nigeria— au stade! Dans ce pays dans lequel lors de son discours de fin d'année, et lors de tous ses discours, le tyran parle comme s'il était Ni John Fru Ndi à propos de son propre bilan catastrophique, accuse le RDPC, accuse les Camerounais, accuse les gens au pouvoir, accuse tout le monde sauf bien sur lui-même (pour cause d'article 53 qui le recouvre d'immunité absolue), le règne du faux maquis s'est installé. Il consiste en ceci: détruire systématiquement le caractère de ceux qui sont justement les critiques du régime, et élever à leur place les clones de la tyrannie c'est-à-dire ceux qui n'accusent jamais le 'chef de l'Etat,' qui accusent plutôt ses collaborateurs de tous les mots, qui trouvent des exutoires au 'président de la république' pour ses incapacités mais vouent aux gémonies 'les sectes' (alors que lui-même est dans plusieurs), ou alors bien sûr, 'les pédés.'

J'ai lu que lorsque les gens (ils n'étaient bien évidemment pas des 'casseurs', noooon, mais 'le peuple'!) qui marchaient derrière le convoi d'Ateba Eyene passaient devant le ministère de Moukoko Mbonjo, ils criaient: 'pédé! pédé! pédé!' Bref, il s'agit d'accuser toute autre personne que le président, et surtout ses collaborateurs, mais bien sûr d'anéantir toute figure critique afin de donner l'illusion que devant le tyran il n'y a rien—nihil, nichts— puis, de substituer à ceux figures néantisées des clones du tyran. Double geste dont l'un est d'anéantissement, et le second de triangulation.

Voilà résumé ce qui se passe au Cameroun de nos jours avec l'élévation d'un scribe et la vaporation d'un chanteur critique, et que quiconque a des yeux pour voir voit— les medias de ce pays sont très faibles, parce que justement ils n'ont pas d'argent (de publicitaires), et parce que les voix critiques ont été chassées du pays depuis belle lurette—les Achille Mbembe, les Célestin Monga, bien sûr les... Lapiro. Cette fabrication du néant critique a trouvé son visage dans la triangulation de medias comme 'Le Messager,' devenu l'ombre de lui-même, car voyez-vous, même le prix Njawe n'existe plus, et son dernier récipiendaire c'était... Paul Biya. Et nous nous rappelons encore les funérailles de Njawe justement au cours desquelles pratiquement une bagarre eut lieu et Célestin Monga fut chassé de la scène publique camerounaise avec son oraison funèbre en poche. Le règne du faux maquis a une bien vieille histoire dans notre pays - datant de ces moments au cours desquels la Guerre civile était chaude. Eh bien, de 1960-1970, des groupes de jeunes étaient montés pour jouer au maquis, habillés comme tel, arme au poing, arrêtés, et présentés aux medias comme des... maquisards. Ils faisaient comme des maquisards, infiltraient le maquis, mais n'étaient pas des maquisards.

Tactique nazie, bien évidemment, dont le maître penseur derrière un sinistre Kame, étaient les Français, comme on dit, et le maître d'oeuvre surtout un certain Semengué. Car la manipulation de l'opinion est un art qui a sa fabrique la plus vieille dans notre pays. Devant nos yeux, elle vient d'avoir lieu avec la néantisation de Lapiro de Mbanga. Evidemment on dira que c'est lui qui 'a choisi de s'exiler' (quand les Charles Ateba Eyene 'se battaient sur le terrain'); on dira que c'est lui qui a choisi de se faire incinérer (quand 'le peuple' se passait le cadavre de Charles Ateba Eyene de main en main et l'élevait au rang de 'héros national'), on l'accusera même d'être lui-même la cause de son cancer quand 'regardez Charles Ateba Eyene, il a été tué parce qu'il critiquait Biya' qui 'n'a pas pu lui trouver 2 millions!' Evidemment on dira que publier une vingtaine d'albums à succès planétaire, et passer trois quatre ans en prison pour rien, n'est rien devant éditer ses livres à compte d'auteur, livres lus seulement au Cameroun, être membre du comité central du RDPC et bavarder dans des radios et télés. On dira que trente ans de carrière à partir de la rue de battant n'est rien devant 'critiquer le pouvoir en étant de la tribu du président'. On dira que Lapiro était déjà vieux, à 56 ans, quand l'autre était un jeune a 46 ans ou quelques. On dira que d'ailleurs même, Lapiro avait 'vendu le peuple', quand l'autre n'a 'jamais trahi le peuple,' lui qui était bien ancien de l'auto-défense sanguinaire, membre du comité central du RDPC et ami intime du général Semengué qui, lui, de son propre aveu coupait les têtes aux Camerounais de 1960-1970 et a présidé ses funérailles. On dira beaucoup de choses, mais le faux maquis se sera révélé dans sa double tactique: néantisation de la critique et triangulation des voix qui pensent justement l'alternative à la tyrannie. Mais surtout le pinacle: substituer le peuple par des clones.

In reaction to Nganang's write-up Bonaventure Tchucham wrote the following mind-boggling piece in *Cameroon Politics* forum:

Matthias Owona Nguini et Le Populisme De Droite

Serais-je à l'étranger que je n'aurais pas cru que l'infamie qui a eu lieu au Cameroun ait vraiment eu lieu— la néantisation de Lapiro de Mbanga, et l'héroisation de Charles Ateba Eyene. Le silence sur le héros national le plus célèbre de ces derniers vingt ans, et l'invention d'un héros national à partir de l'écume de la droite. Et que celle-ci fut orchestrée par une décision extraordinaire— celle d'un qu'on me dit spécialiste de sciences politiques— Matthias Owona Nguini. Avec l'arrestation de Bapes Bapes, nous passons à autre chose. Le Cameroun aura donc passé sous silence le décès de Lapiro de Mbanga, ses funérailles, et tout ce qu'il aura été— Lapiro! Lapiro! Lapiro! Trente ans de musique auront ainsi été mis dans le silence d'une indignation, quand la meute astroturfée prenait la rue, avec devant elle Matthias Owona Nguini. Je dois dire que je n'ai jamais cru qu'il soit une force de changement. Son péché originel m'a toujours mis sur les gardes. Mais ce qui m'a toujours fait douter est qu'il ait toujours manqué le courage d'un jugement. Je précise ma pensée: un intellectuel, c'est une analyse, basée elle sur un jugement, qui se fonde dans un paradigme précis. Trois piliers dont le premier forme des universitaires. Bref, il m'est toujours apparu comme un universitaire, jetant le jargon de sa discipline à la télévision pour éblouir, ce qui a lieu évidemment. La lignée de Mbembe, quoi.

Le jugement se situe, lui dans le feu de l'action, car alors il faut choisir. Et là l'analyste chez l'homme a toujours servi de poche d'esquive— ce qu'au pays on appelle 'l'objectivitéî.' Ainsi jamais ne s'est-il soucié de ses étudiants incarcérés, même quand c'était tout à fait évident que ceux-ci étaient innocents, été contrepartie étaient jetés dans des prisons aussi infames que Mfou—Herve Nzoubeth, Denis Emillien Atangana, Demanga sont des exemples les plus infames de sa fuite quand l'histoire de son propre amphi appelait le jugement. Ce qui cependant s'est joué à Yaoundé ces derniers jours révèle le jugement autant que le paradigme duquel il part - car l'héroïsation de Charles Ateba Eyene demeure pour moi extraodinaire, et encore plus indigestible, parce qu'elle est assise sur le silence de la république sur la mort et l'enterrement d'un homme, Lapiro de Mbanga, qui aura passé 55 de ses 56 ans au Cameroun, et qui sera mort en exil, oui, mort en exil, après avoir passé 4 de ces 56 ans-là en prison pour rien! Voilà bien cet homme que durant sa vie la rue aura porté, aura questionné, aura suivi, aura défendu au final, et qui sera mort loin d'elle - comme tant de héros de ce pays!

Mais ce qui est le plus troublant pour moi, plus troublant même que le silence sur l'héroisme de Lapiro de Mbanga, c'est le choix de Charles Ateba Eyene, l'apôtre du ressentiment comme 'héros national'. Quoi? Quel choix écervelé! Lever les foules en jetant en pâture 'les éperviables' fait déjà le 'héros national' au Cameroun? Comment célébrer telle écume, quand je viens de passer un après-midi avec un de ces hommes qui a passé cinq ans en prison à Kondengui, et a été innocenté totalement dans ce Cameroun par le tribunal spécial devant lequel il a démontré son innocence justement, comme Lapiro avait démontré devant la Cour suprême la sienne et fut innocenté? Comment célébrer ceux qui voient 'les pédés' partout dans leur misère, qui criminalisent le succès, qui se retournent contre l'excellence au nom des 'sectes'? C'est ça l'héroisme au Cameroun? Vraiment? Ça fait pitié! Le ressentiment, oui, c'est cela, et ce n'a jamais rien produit de bon, rien, rien, et rien. Voyez donc, chez nous ce sont 'les éperviables', 'les pédés', et ailleurs ce sont 'les juifs,' 'les noirs' qui sont la cause des malheurs de la race. Elever le pire des poujadismes au rang d'héroisme dans ce pays, quand celui-ci est au creu de la tyrannie, ah quelle déroute intellectuelle! Il a parlé de 'vérité'. La vérité dans ce Cameroun de la tyrannie c'est ça vraiment, le ressentiment? Ah, me dit-on, que Charles Ateba Eyene c'était son ami, sinon venait de l'Océan comme lui - c'est à se demander si c'est ainsi que notre professeur corrige ses copies. Donne les meilleures notes à ses copains, ou alors aux gens de sa tribu. Juste parce qu'il le peut. Ah, le pays organisateur! Ah, le pays organisateur! Les même gens, les même méthodes!

Another reaction to Nganang's article is written by Chief Charles A. Taku in the *Cameroon Politics* forum:

Patrice,

Your posting puts in perspective the battle for the soul of Cameroun.

Lapiro spent his life championing the cause of freedom and liberty and died for the cause. He leaves an enduring legacy that transcends the boundaries of neo-colonial Cameroun. The sheer number of thesis and studies conducted in centres of excellence in learning worldwide on his artistic works moves him to the level of Fela and others. But the struggle that Lapiro now eternalizes is part of a larger conundrum that the forces of neo-colonialism and tyranny continue to wedge against the soul of Africa. Jacob Nguni, a childhood friend of Lapiro and fellow musician has already proclaimed that Lapiro is greater now that he is by the side of his creator than alive; and that those who may think that without Lapiro they can sacrifice the hopes and aspirations of the citizenry must rethink their folly. He is right. Yes indeed, he is right.

I wrote a eulogy for Atebe Eyene for a reason different from those of the oppressive forces he served. My eulogy was about his public attack on mystical orders and secret societies and their influence on the governance of neo-colonial Republic of Cameroun under the supposed new deal government. I praised his courage in so doing but pointed out that his attempt to blame all but Paul Biya was disingenuous and futile since Paul Biya bears the ultimate command responsibility for the acts and conducts of his subordinates. However, no matter what perception the gullible public may think about the public statements of Ateba Eyene , question marks will always paint his legacy for attempting to whitewash Paul Biya for the misrule that has rocked the very foundation of the "Etat Garnison" that Lapiro questioned even before any one else had the courage to openly speak about.

The Cameroun Press you have written about lost its credibility to the advantage of Lapiro whose message of freedom is enduring. The campaign of calumny orchestrated against Lapiro trailed some of us who are committed to forging ahead with the battle for the soul of the poor and the weak which Lapiro now eternalizes and which he discussed with us with the pedagogic alacrity of a genuine professor. It is when the dust will settle after this weekend burials that the poor and the weak will review the life and times of persons who claimed to speak for the majority poor and died in so doing. It is in so doing that Lapiro and his enduring legacy will stand out as the sole and uncontested platform for genuine freedom and liberty. For now, the scene you have described is but a sign of desperation of the majority poor that is hungry and tasting to have the liberating spirit of Lapiro fearful of a life without him. But the spirit of Lapiro will live to direct them towards the goals he lived, fought and died for come a hundred years as Celestine Monga predicted in his eulogy in that Church in New York today.

Lapiro's last public appearance was in Washington DC barely a few months ago in an event in which I was a guest speaker. His presence on that occasion and his performance thereafter in a public event attended by thousands who carried him shoulder high beat all records as those who attended may testify. He informed me that many persons advised him against attending the event and some chastised him for his determination despite his condition to attend nevertheless. He informed me that after an intense reflection, he convinced himself that his presence in honor of the invitation would contribute in resolving the contentious issues confronting the people he loved so much. Additionally,

119

he convinced himself that he hoped to make a statement by his participation that he was one of us after all.

For these reasons, he gave his last honor to this constituency and elicited some of the recorded very emotional and heartfelt acclamation any Cameroonian has had in recent memory. The videos of his presence and thereafter his performance will be passed from generation to generation; so also his participation and contribution. In this event as many others in his recorded career since he began his musical career in Soul Jungle in Victoria, then Central Bar in Muyuka, and then Kumba where his soul mate and life long friend Jacob Nguni testifies were always dedicated to drawing attention to the plight of the poor and the weak and the ills afflicting society, Lapiro made a point, which is not lost on all of us.

May God bless the soul of Lapiro and his enduring struggle for freedom which must prevail.

Chief Charles A. Taku

Mishe Fon who personally sponsored a bus trip to New York for the burial of Lapiro de Mbanga wrote the following piece. It appeared in the *Camnetwork* forum:

The New York trip 4 the burial of Lapiro de Mbanga na daso six hours by "American Guaranty Express." The weather according to accurate "mungang" forecast will be "nice and warm." To show our solidarity with this Musical icon, I suggest every cultural group should be represented. Given our demographics in the DMV (Washington) area we should be travelling to New York with more than three buses. Don't be afraid to put your name on the list. None of those useless njim-tetes in Yaounde will touch one single biabia on your kongolibong crobeaux heads. I know many Cameroonians would have loved for their idol LAPIRO de

MBANGA to be buried in grand style in his city of adoption MBANGA or DOUALA and why not even in YAOUNDE....but ih dey as ih dey. The Repe langua we say make dem enterer yi for Amellika. We, his extended family, are merely respecting the desiderata and instructions of the fallen hero. For that reason alone; those of us who are opportune to be here at this time, should come out in our numbers to pay the guy our befitting last respects. See you all in the Bus-Ride. I will be selling "Merecine 4 Sugar Sugar, Montolli, High Brod Pleasure, Die-Betisse, Kam No Go, Craw Craw, See-Philipps, Njang-Bin deny 4 tanap and even HIV-Eights" in the bus throughout the "aller-retour" trip. Come One Come all.

Mishe Fon

One of Cameroon's literary virtuosos, Bill Ndi, poeticizes the death of Lapiro de Mbanga in the following ode in *Cameroon Politics* forum:

Our Case
Kill our earthly stars.
What will you do to the heavenly ones?
To protect yourself, grease the soldiers' beard.
What shall you do when at your door death knocks?
Bring us the Opposition in a coffin.
But will you let us freely mourn?
You kill our poets.
Do you believe we will bury their writings?
Bury yourself amidst a zillion soldiers.
Haven't you learned from Chinese History?
Like you, in China one did this.
Did he not rot underground?
You sum your world with Law and Order.

Why let lawlessness and disorderliness reign?
You are god to those who buy your favours.
Who or what are you to those you strip of basic rights?
Every night, you go to sleep on a king size bed.
Why not make your heart the size of your bed?
You ruin the nation to live in a mansion.
What space in it or our minds do you occupy?
You've dominated the nation tyrannically.
Shall you ever be the tyrant that kills death?
We thought to rule was to serve.
Why must a tyrant like you be served?
Now, to yourself, you've gathered the nation's wealth?
  Won't you give us the right to determine the future of
  our misery?
You push your tyranny, your greed and grip on power to
the last.
Won't you still be proven wrong from beginning and end?
You may never stand in front of any court to plead guilty.
But which other criminal supersedes you?
With your sentence as long as life,
Shall you in your dead bed rule over us?
You may never see this as a case.
But, here, are we not free to rest our case?

Bill Ndi

As tribute to Lapiro, Vakunta transcribes an excerpt from
the musical virtuoso's latest album *Démissionnez*!:

Hommage à un combattant
Ancien chaud gars na mouilleur!
Step down! Démissionnez!
Because you dong over massacré constitution…

You dong over échouer
Subordination du pouvoir judiciaire na you!
Subordination du pouvoir législatif na you!
Manoeuvre politique avec impunité na soso you!
Step down! Démissionnez!
Because you dong over mouiller!
Insécurité généralisée—
Chavoum dong hala for banque for Bonaberi
Fusils dong hala for Pont de Wouri
Dem dong meng your chef de terre,
Kamambrou for Bakassi
You dong over mouiller!
Step down! Démissionnez!
Ngeme and chômage
Dong multiplié for dis mboko
Bendskinneurs, chauffeurs clandos,
Laveurs de voitures, tackleurs, sauveteurs
Bayam sellams, coiffeurs and coiffeuses ambulantes
For Marché Central, call-boxeurs...
Dem di pointer na for dong rain and for dong sun...
Preuve, dem di kick muna bébés
For maternité everywhere for we own kondre.
No be youa boulot na sécurisation
Des personnes et de leurs biens?
A vrai dire this one na échec total
If you no fit garantir sécurité sep for nourrissons!
Step down! Démissionnez! You dong over mouiller!

Another endearing poem comes from Christmas Ebini:

Albert, Reuben, Ernest, Pius and Lapiro
Do you know anyone here
Who has heard of my good friend Albert Mukong

A man I call my political father
Who spent his life fighting for freedom
Shaming the French and evil neocolonialist
And was prisoner without a crime?
Can you tell me what you know about him?
For I just went on exile and he was gone
He stood for a lot of good, equality and justice
As it seems the good and brave die early

Does anybody here
Know of anyone who knows Reuben Um Nyobé
A brave warrior, patriot and nationalist
Who courageously said no to demonic France
As they refused to leave our beloved land
Making a sham of what they called independence
Placing their stooges to plunder our land
Chasing and silencing our national hero
Fighting courageously even to death
And yet before I was of age to think
He was gone and a monument of my memory
As it seems the good and brave die young and early?

Has anyone here
Seen or heard of our friend and father Ernest Ouandie?
Before I could grow up he was taken from us
Deprived from joining his nationalism spirit
And his determination to keep France out
Caging the betrayals of political stooges
Who sold the nation for neo-colonial games
He bravely fought for our independence and freedom
But before we could turn around he was gone
And became an imprint in our national psyche
As it seems the good and the brave die young and early.

Has anybody here
Seen my good old friend and brother Pius Njawe
He stood for and fought many good causes
For our freedom, our justice and our integrity
But before I could hold his hand he was gone
Taken from us just when we needed him most
Can someone please tell me where he's gone
For it seems the good and the brave die young and early.

Has anyone here been to Buffalo
Did you see our hero Lapiro
Was he looking happy or sad?
He stood for and fought many good causes
Same as Albert, Reuben, Ernest and Pius
But before I could turn around to put facts together
That he is and was not LP Judas of M he was gone
Taken away from me holding his hands to say I know
The tricks of the real devil and the devils in sheep
clothing
For I know now only the good and brave die young and
early.

Has anybody here
Seen me seeking for the brave and good ones
Who amongst us will take the mantle to lead
To wear the armor of goodness and bravery
Of Albert, Reuben, Ernest, Pius and Lapiro
Who here would not love the things they stood for
Did they not try to find and do some good?
For you, me, us, our nation, our people and our world
As they started out to set us and our land free
And from their works and memory and sacrifices
We will be free soon and someday when we choose

And I thought I saw Lapiro holding hands over Fako
Mountain
With Albert, Reuben, Ernest and our good friend Pius
Singing and praying for us not to forget their sacrifices
As they have just gone home and watching over us
As it seems the good and brave die young and early.

Christmas Ebini

The selfsame Ebini wrote the following piece published *in Cameroon Politics:*

For those who were not aware or privileged to feel the impact of what Lapiro meant or symbolized to the Cameroonian struggle for freedom and justice for the downtrodden, please read the poem below I wrote about him in the 90s. This was when it was alleged that he had betrayed the hopes and admirations people like myself had for him. I have said it many times and I will say it again: Lapiro to a person of my thinking was the most authentic and relevant Cameroonian of our time. I felt blessed to know that such a person existed in a land I was a part of; a country where everyone (the highly educated and saintly amongst us) saw evil and either looked the other way with pathetic silence or became willing collaborators to it. Mark you that I had just returned from the United States a couple of years back with an MBA and joined the civil service as an economics teacher and Lapiro was the only Cameroonian who spoke to my soul and gave me hope that something can be done to challenge the evil that existed in that land. His resolve and courage emboldened me and for those who knew me, I took significant risks as a civil servant without fear of arrest, imprisonment or even death.

So you can understand how depressed one could get when the words came out that this man whom I held in so high esteem had collaborated with the devil to kill the great revolution he started. At that time, George Ngwane, Bate Besong, myself and others had added to our activism the art of reaching people through writing. I wrote my first poem in jail in Ekondo Titi while in detention with George Ngwane and two other teachers after we wrote a booklet title VIEWPOINTS, criticizing the government and the president. So it was just natural for me to deal with my disappointment towards Lapiro's fall through the poem bellow. It is a shame that those who knew the facts then did not speak out for whatever reason but allowed Lapiro to carry such a mark on him and a cross for so long. It is truly regrettable that some of them are only speaking after this great soul has been carefully destroyed and killed. For them too I will write a poem.

Please watch the link below to the end to hear what I said about Lapiro in the 90s and connect to the poem.

This is what I will say to Lapiro to show my gratitude as he sleeps: NO DAY SHALL ERASE YOU FROM THE MEMORY OF TIME AS LONG AS I LIVE.

Good night great warrior.

Christmas Ebini then wrote the following poem:

LP Judas of M
Your voice echoed in the wilderness
Crying out what was forbidden
Challenging a hard-hearted Midas
Against a ruthless barbaric dynasty

Your message was in our hearts

127

For we thought you fought for us
Being on our side in the struggle
Against an inflicted virus

We praised your efforts
We hailed your names
Knowing greater men than you
Could not fight on our side

You from complete emptiness
And a very humble standing
Would dare to stand for us
And sing and speak against the king

Money and titles could not buy you
The esteem we reserved you
Like the one villains get
With force and intimidation

Now we know who you really are
A Judas pretending to be a savior
For the light has shown in the darkness
And caught you unawares
In the act of negotiating
To sell those you pretended to love
To the very enemies you so well criticized

Oh complice LP Judas of M
How much is it worth
To sell away our love and friendship
How much are you paid
To negotiate our death warrants
And betray us to our enemies?

As sure as justice must prevail
And much as our struggle must continue
You will live to regret
The devil you have worshipped
And wish you were never born
Just as Judas your master

Boh Herbert's moving testimony is powerful enough to draw tears from the most callous biped that ever walked the surface of this earth. It was published in the *Camnetwork* forum as follows:

Dear All,

It is perhaps not my place to send out this message of thanks to the many Lapiro fans, friends and family who traveled to Buffalo, New York, over the weekend from across the world (mourners came from as far out as London) but also from across the United States and Canada to bid "Ndinga Man" safe travels into glory and to condole with his family.

No one has delegated me to send this message, except that the spirit moves me and I think it would be foolish not to heed the calling of the spirit. Lapiro has warned us against acting foolish: "Mbout na sick!"

It may ring queer to the ear to hear those who made the trip or watched online say of this "die" that it was good. Well - that is just the truth. Lapiro's "die" this weekend was great! Everything came together: turnout, eulogies, honors, respect, grieving, consolation, singing, song and dance, etc. "Ndinga Man" must be smiling from beyond the grave.

Thanks to one and all, but special thanks to our "big" brother Jacob Nguni, who was excellent in the roles of chief mourner and lead eulogist, despite the pain of our loss. Thanks to the leadership and members of ACCDF, who in my opinion best symbolized through their bus ride this weekend that several waves of pilgrims shall come to Buffalo henceforth in pilgrimage, recognizing the city not only as the city on the banks of the Niagara Falls, famous for its Buffalo Wild Wings, but now as the final home and resting place of the hero, Lapiro.

How can anyone say thanks enough to Lapiro's family, especially his widow Loisette and the children, as well as his sisters and brothers, who bore their pain with courage, dignity and trust in Christ's promise of the resurrection so eloquently articulated by Loisette at the close of the Requiem Mass when she spoke of the coming of many more Lapiros.

Thanks to the Cameroonian community of Buffalo, the sister community of Cameroonians of Toronto, Canada, who crossed the Niagara in their numbers to help make the funeral a success, and thanks to the leadership and parishioners of the St. Gregory the Great Catholic Church for lifting Lapiro and his family to God in their thoughts and prayers.

Lapiro Lives! Lapiro Forever!

Boh Herbert

This piece speaks volumes about the aura that surrounded mourners in Buffalo New York:

By Folefac Richard in Buffalo, New York USA

Hundreds of Family, friends, well-wishers and international human rights advocates were present on Friday and Saturday March 28-29 2014 in Buffalo, New York for the last funeral rites for musician Lambo Pierre Roger Sanjo aka Lapiro de Mbanga.

Lapiro, sing my own song

Speakers during the two day funeral that included a wake and church service at the St Gregory the Great Roman Catholic Church in Willaimsville (Buffalo, NY) included World Bank Journalist Boh Herbert, Sidony Sandjo, Lapiro's step-sister, former Student leader Corantin Talla and guitarist Jacob Nguni, a close friend and confidant of Lapiro. Louisette Noukeu, Lapiro's wife also spoke during his funeral calling on mourners to pray for the repose of the soul of her husband and father of her children.

Boh Herbert told the mourners that Lapiro left an indelible mark in Cameroon and will never be forgotten. Like Lapiro, he called on those left behind to emulate his example in fighting against injustice in Cameroon "Plan so that even in death, they will not triumph and I want to applaud Lapiro because he has not given them one chance to triumph even in his death. I salute you big brother" Herbert said to applause from the mourners.

Sidonie Sandjo, step-sister of Lapiro who flew in from Paris for the funeral said her brother more than anyone in their large family, made them proud and known around the world through his music and fight for the respect of the rights of everyone. She said the family was blessed and will forever miss him. Lapiro's father, Sandjo Roger Blanchard, was a well-known wealthy businessman.

Close friend, confidant and fellow musician Jacob Nguni recounted his life-long friendship with Lapiro saying the world had lost a great man who in death, was now bigger than he was alive.

World Bank economist Celestin Monga recounted how Lapiro bravely organized protest marches following his and journalist Pius Njawe's 1991 arrest and detention for writing and publishing a newspaper editorial considered insulting to long-serving president Paul Biya. He was also categorical Lapiro's memory will live on in the collective consciousness of all Cameroonians.

Former student leader Corantin Talla said on record claims the government henchman Jean Forchive paid Lapiro to betray the opposition in 1991 were untrue. Mr. Talla worked closely with Lapiro and other human right activists during the university uprisings in the early 90's.

Bidding a star goodbye

In a brief chat with *Iroko Magazine* following the funeral, Jacob Nguni said it was heart breaking none of the politicians, including SDF Chairman John Fru Ndi, a comrade in arms whom he supported, bothered to send condolence messages following his demise. "Cameroonian politics, fight for human rights and freedom cannot be written without a mention of Lapiro," Mr Nguni added. He said he was proud to be a friend and brother of Lapiro and was extremely happy when his funeral attracted foreigners some of whom only heard about the man and his music after his death. His said Lapiro used his music to expose the weaknesses of the political class in Cameroon and in the end, made the ultimate sacrifice for the people.

As expected, some of Lapiro's best known songs were played during the wake keeping that held on March 28, 2014. A grand celebration of the life of Lapiro is now being planned and will take place in Washington D.C in a venue that will be announced soon.

Sadly enough, Lapiro's death has also sparked a flurry of disconcerting write-ups in Cameroonian online forums like *Cameroon Politics* and *Camnetwork*. This goes to show that our hero, Lapiro de Mbanga, was not a terrestrial god; he was only human. The contentious pieces such as the one written by Jacob Nguni follow:

People,

Before December 31, 1989, Mr. John Fru Ndi was a relatively unknown bookseller in the town of Bamenda. His name meant nothing to the common Cameroonian out of the township of Bamenda. On that particular night of December 31, 1989, Mr. John Fru Ndi most probably did not know what destiny had in store for him, politically speaking. He had been a CNU member and was still inkling with the same CNU that had metamorphosed into the CPDM a few years back right there in the town of Bamenda.

Somewhere in Cameroon on that same day, December 31, 1989, a prominent musician going by the stage name Lapiro de Mbanga was preparing for a huge New Year's eve concert in downtown Douala, 192 miles away from Bamenda. It would be none of Mr. John Fru Ndi's business as he, like many other "responsible" Cameroonians at the time, was not really connected with the type of music that Lapiro was known for and surtout the type of language of the so-labeled dregs of society that was the medium of communication between Lapiro and his millions of fans of "low-class" folks around the country.

On the night of December 31, 1989, while Lapiro was busy on stage singing about the plight of the poor and the downtrodden in our country, Mr. John Fru Ndi was getting ready to go to bed after 2 or 3 cups of overnight mbu that he had gulped down at a small obscure house party with his fellow mbu drinkers to usher in the New Year 1990. On that night Mr. John Fru and Lapiro had nothing in common, had never met before and had no plans to meet as both of them were full strangers to one another with the only difference being that Mr. John Fru Ndi must have surely heard about Lapiro whereas Lapiro surely knew nothing about John Fru Ndi on this particular night.

Come January 1, 1990 and beyond, the political wind of change that started sweeping across Africa got hold of Cameroon and many things began to happen. From nowhere emerged a political party known as the SDF with a relatively unknown John Fru Ndi as the chairman. The grapevine had it that the founders of the SDF were staunched members of the CPDM who took to the back seat in the beginning and shunned the position of chairman because they feared reprisals from the Yaounde regime. This fear of reprisals by the staunch founding fathers is what led to the bold but unprepared Mr. John Fru Ndi to be (s) elected as the pioneer, cum self-proclaimed "life", chairman of the SDF.

Be it as it may, the launching of the SDF in Bamenda was greeted with some hostility by the Yaounde regime and the fact that Mr. John Fru Ndi was chairman left the Yaounde regime consternated as they could not figure out who John Fru Ndi was and why he was chosen as Chairman. This confusion is what led the government to go back to the drawing board to find out those who were actually calling the shots in the SDF and the void created by this inaction on the part of the government gave room for the SDF to find its feet on the ground.

However, the SDF started making waves and came to be accepted as a party to be reckoned with. That notwithstanding, this was also the time that the UNDP led by former P.M. Bello Bouba and the UDC led by Mr. Ndam Njoya were rising to prominence. These two political opposition parties were up there and the regime was not taking any chances. At this precise moment, the Yaounde regime was focused on the UNDP and the UDC because their chairmen were men of substance and also former close collaborators of the chairman of the ruling CPDM party. A name like John Fru Ndi was not seen as a threat to the regime as such despite the fact that death had occurred in the streets of Bamenda during its launching.

At that time in 1990, Lapiro de Mbanga had more supporters than all the political parties combined including the CPDM. Lapiro had risen to become the voice of the voiceless and the real champion of change in Cameroon. Whereas the UNDP had a northern Cameroon tone to its structure, the UDC with a Noun departmental tone to its structure, the UPC with a Bassa tone to its structure and finally the SDF with a graffi tone to its structure, Lapiro's constituency cut across tribal lines.

Yes, Lapiro's constituency cut across the length and breadth of Cameroon, defying all tribal connotations. Lapiro's constituency had no constitution. Lapiro's constituency had no NEC. Lapiro's constituency had no political setup or organizational chart. Lapiro's constituency had no treasurer. Lapiro's constituency had no attorneys at law. Lapiro's constituency had no offices. Lapiro's constituency had no chairman.

Lapiro's constituency was the people. Lapiro's constituency was the downtrodden. Lapiro's constituency was the poor. Lapiro's constituency was the abused and denigrated. Lapiro's constituency looked up to him as the messiah for change. They revered Lapiro. They loved him. They liked him. They loved his music. And in his music, they found their lost dignity or whatever was left of it. Lapiro became the man who could make or mar anyone in the opposition. He became the first to have the last say. By default, Lapiro became the kingmaker.

It was for all the above reasons that at the onset of multiparty politics in Cameroon in 1990, which was more than 5 years after Lapiro had been on the scene as the only voice of the voiceless, all the opposition political parties in Cameroon did all their underground biddings to get Lapiro's endorsement. That is what it was and nobody can deny this fact. He who was going to win Lapiro's endorsement was surely going to outshine the others and carry the day. At the end of the day, the SDF party won Lapiro's endorsement and the SDF party moved from being a basically graffi entity to a powerful national party.

As a consequence, Mr. John Fru Ndi who had now assumed the title of "Ni" John Fru Ndi became the direct beneficiary of Lapiro's endorsement putting him ahead of renowned political power horses like Bouba Bello Maigari of the UNDP, Ndam Njoya of the UDC and whoever that Bassa fellow was of the tattered UPC. The SDF rose to prominence as all Lapiro's supporters became members of the SDF and Ni John Fru Ndi became the symbol of Cameroon's opposition overnight without lifting a pound.

There is no Cameroonian out there who can remember one thing that Fru Ndi said he would do differently if voted to power. No internal or external policies were ever tabled or sold by the SDF. "SDF, Power" is all that was echoed and re-echoed and still being re-echoed to this day that it has become a cracked record. That is what I meant by Fru Ndi becoming what he became without lifting a pound. I cannot hate myself for being a member of the SDF at that time because we all thought that anything was better than the CPDM. We were wrong and regrettably so wrong.

Anyway, I do not want to go into that which transpired between 1990 and the time Lapiro suffered persecution from members of the opposition and the state security service jointly and severally. For now, I will also skip the role that opposition leaders played in that saga. All that will be dealt with at some point. I do not also want to go into what led to Lapiro's incarceration that subsequently became the beginning of his imminent demise. Let me not even get into the deportment and/or reaction of our so-called opposition political leaders when the verdict of 3 years was handed down.

Let's keep in mind that the prosecutor of the case that sentenced Lapiro to three years in jail was one Helen Fon-Achu, a Justice by rank, who had actually asked that Lapiro be sentenced to 10 to 20 years along with a fine of 280 million francs. Here is an excerpt of the prosecutor Helen Fon-Achu's submission in court:

> State prosecutor Justice Helen Fon-Achu said it openly in the court room on 24 June 2009, in the hours before the musician was convicted. According to her, "Lapiro should be given an exemplary and dissuasive sanction in order to intimidate those who would try to repeat such act." So, she asked for a 10 to 20 years jail sentence for him.

However, the presiding bench had a hard time making a decision and it took them 10 hours to decide on the 3-year sentence. It would have normally taken them less than 3 hours but they found themselves between a rock and a hard place. It is even rumored that two of the judges had found Lapiro not guilty and were at worse going to put him on probation but prosecutor Justice Helen Fon-Achu was adamant and wanted Lapiro to serve jail time at all costs. Self-interest?

Justice Helen Fon-Achu later got rewarded for her role in putting Lapiro in jail and now finds herself in Buea as a

High Court Judge. I hope Justice Helen Fon-Achu should be happy now that Lapiro is gone to sleep. I am sure Lapiro forgave her as he has never mentioned her name since he left jail. Let God bless Justice Helen Fon-Achu and take her out of the darkness in which she finds herself.

Fast forward to March 16, 2014. Lapiro left this world to the great beyond at 11:35 a.m. EST on Sunday March 16, 2014 in Buffalo, NY, USA. The news of Lapiro's passing spread like wild fire across the globe within minutes. Some Cameroonians in the USA actually got the news from sources in Cameroon. It was all over the place that Lapiro de Mbanga AKA Ndinga Man was gone.

From Sunday March 16, 2014 to the day of Lapiro's funeral on March 28/29, 2014 and to this minute I am penning this down, not one word, not one communique, not one condolence message to the press or to the family has been issued by Ni John Fru Ndi, chairman of the SDF and the man who owes his one-time popularity to Lambo Sandjo Pierre Roger AKA Lapiro de Mbanga. The last we heard from Ni John Fru Ndi was his complaint of the way he was shabbily treated by Paul Biya's security service during the ceremony of whatever was happening in Buea. Na who send yi? I do not have a single word to add apart from saying that you be the judge. I rest my case right here.

Jacob Nguni

Dear Mr. Nguni,

I have been absent from the forum for some time and may not exactly know what has been going on. As I tried to reconnect today, I came across your article on Fru Ndi and Lapiro. I wish to state that I was a bit taken aback by some inaccuracies which are not characteristic of your postings.

I would suggest that you review the section concerning the prosecution of Lapiro in Douala. There are too many inaccuracies concerning the prosecutor, the judges and the positions they hold today. You may have been misled by newspaper articles and rumors. I think that if you cite the name of somebody, then the subsequent information about that person should be as near accurate as possible.

May I also submit that the assertion that Lapiro transformed the SDF from a graffi party to a national party is very incorrect. That assertion is not backed by any empirical data. I, therefore, join issues with Mr. Ekinneh in discountenancing most of the encomiums that you poured on Lapiro.

I do not know if you intentionally forgot or left out the fact that Lapiro dined with Fochive and thereafter described the action of opposition leaders as irresponsible.

My own records show that Lapiro rose to prominence during the trial of Celestin Monga and Pius Njawe. He used to rally crowds and march round the court house in Douala. Prior to that period, he was just an obscure vulgar musician who appealed to the *bas peuple* because of the similitude between his music and their life style. My conclusion is that Fru Ndi owes no special tribute to Lapiro more than he owes to any other dead Cameroonian. I will revisit this article to see about the corrections you have made about the trial of Lapiro in Douala. As Pa Fru Ndeh used to say, I have intimate details about many Cameroonians.

Bens Awaah

Bens,

NESPROG or NESCAFE is without relevance to my point that you are trying to obfuscate. I know that some of you cannot get over your tribalistic approach to anything written here. I have asked you, the defender of whatever you want to defend, to tell me why Fru Ndi has been missing in action since Lapiro's passing and you are hiding under the table using NESPROG and NESCAFE as an umbrella.

Let me tell you that I, as a member of the SDF and a staunch supporter of Ni John Fru Ndi's in the peak of the wind of change in Cameroon, you have nothing to tell me about that party. We are the ones who composed the songs that were sung in the streets in Kumba, Southwest in those days. And for that I was invited to Ntarikon Park.

I spent a whole week in Bamenda paying my hotel bills off pocket. I was picked up every morning for Ntarikon wherefrom we headed to the rally grounds where those Takumbengs always sat on the ground as the Chairman spoke. At that time, the Chairman had a bandage on his right foot for a wound he got from a shooting around Mbouda. The Chairman was to meet again with me during his visit to Kumba.

I personally took a lot of risks in Kumba supporting the SDF in a town that the Mukete Gang had held a good part hostage. You cannot tell me anything about the SDF. I took the risk of offering my 8,000-watt P. A. system for the SDF rally to hold in Kumba Town Green after law enforcement agents had gone around town to warn all discotheque owners not to hire their stuff.

Before the rally began, SONEL cut off power to the same Town Green and I rushed home to bring my power generator. That was very risky because Town Green is out of the SDF enclave in Kumba. The fact that some of you come here making noise about politics does not mean *shege* because it is obvious why you in particular supported the SDF.

I also met with the Chairman during one of his US visits in 2000. You were, at most, a distant supporter of the SDF as much as you are now of the SCNC. I know the real SCNC people whom I can handle a level headed discussion with and not bare-faced wind blowing fanatics like you, sir. Do not try to belittle a late guy who you never knew, okay.

Let's leave out the way the SDF used to function and focus on my observation, which is the deafening silence of Ni John Fru Ndi since the passing of Lapiro. Do not try to play any kontri-man game with me because you are not more graffi than myself. Did you help in selling NESPROG? Have you in particular ever read that doki?

If you do not have anything to say about my observation, then stay there and enjoy your NESPROG or NESCAFE, whichever comes first.

Jacob Nguni

Dear Micro,

I would start by thanking you for the invitation to attend the occasion of the celebration of the life of Lapiro. That said, I think you got me wrong completely on what I said about your write up on Lapiro. Maybe we may understand each other better if I go specific. You wrote that, " prosecutor Justice Helen Fon-Achu was adamant and wanted Lapiro to be served jail time at all costs. Self-interest?

You added that, Justice Helen Fon-Achu later got rewarded for her role in putting Lapiro in jail and now finds herself in Buea as a High Court Judge." Micro, you never took time to verify those facts before putting them down in writing. Firstly, Justice Helen Fon-Achu only came in contact with the case of Lapiro after Lapiro had been convicted by a lower court. It was in the course of an appeal made by Lapiro himself that Justice Helen Fon entered appearance in her capacity as the advocate General of the Littoral Region to make her submissions in what is known as "les réquisitions du ministère public". What is very clear is that she had no self-interest in her submissions to the court.

Secondly, the reward of going to Buea as a High Court judge following the imprisonment of Lapiro is not true. Justice Helen Fon was never posted to Buea High Court. It would have instead been a punishment if she left from the court of appeal of the littoral to a high court. That, in effect, is a demotion.

Contrary to your view that I hold Lapiro in disdain, I want to tell you that my two best Cameroon musicians are Petit Pays and Lapiro. Can you hold that which you like in disdain? My answer is no. Politically, Lapiro and I never shared the same philosophy, but I had a lot of respect for him when he rallied the crowds to clamor for the liberation of Celestin Monga and Njawe. I was dispatched from Yaounde to go down to Douala and work with the state prosecutor, Nantchouang Daniel. Unfortunately for me, Monga was my friend, but I had to ensure that the submissions of the State Counsel were compatible with what the law required. The person who could have done anything good for them was the presiding judge, Fongang. Maybe I would give more details when I come back from honoring the invitation of Micro.

Georges Jules Owona

Mr. Agbaw,

When was "Mimba we" released? To wit, you are the one trying to reinvent history. I stand by what I said and it is a verifiable fact. Believe what you want, spread all what you want but the truth is that Lapiro was in the fight long before all our so-called opposition leaders came to the scene. And of all the opposition leaders who stepped out in 1990, the one figure who indeed benefitted from Lapiro's popularity was Ni John Fru Ndi of the SDF. You can take that to any bank, any day, anytime.

If you can manage to answer my first question to you, you will find out how wrong you are. To my own consternation, I am here telling a historical fact about Ni John Fru Ndi and Lapiro and the fact that Fru Ndi has been quiet since the passing of Lapiro and here you come, injecting the names of other political figures whom I have nothing to do with because I do not see them in the same light as much as you do. Yes, some came out but coming out for something is one thing whereas having an impact like Lapiro did is quite another. No belittlement by you or people who think like you can change the facts. FYI, I was not out of the country at the time you are talking about.

Above all, the crux of my write-up of this morning is the fact that Ni John Fru Ndi has been missing in action since the passing of Lapiro. If you have any justification for Ni Fru Ndi's deafening silence, then please go ahead and tell us. That being said, I see your reaction as some form of obfuscation on your part.

I do not know whether you ever spoke to Lapiro on any topic. There are many stories out there. I wonder whether you know the roles that some of the names you mentioned in your mail had to do with the devilish calculated attempt to bring down Lapiro. I think you are talking about some of these people based on how you knew/know them and not because you really knew/know them.

Ask Njeukam C. whom you mentioned in your mail to come out today and talk about the different fictitious figures that he and his fellow plotters against Lapiro sat down in a meeting and decided they should use as the amount of money that Fochive had given Lapiro. Njeukam and

Co debated on using 15 million FCFA or 30 million FCFA but finally decided they should use 22 million FCFA as the sum that Lapiro was paid with by Fochive Jean.

The Romans simply took advantage of the hatred and jealousy that some "powerful" Jews had for Jesus Christ. Lapiro was almost brought down by his own Bami brothers who saw him as a threat to the huge benefits they were making from the sale of so-called "Carton Rouge" that he Lapiro was totally against. The real story behind the "Sovereign Natonal Conference has never been told but some of us knew that it really had nothing to do with changing Cameroon but everything to do with personal interests, which Lapiro was against and as such, he had to be brought down by any means.

Let Njeukam come out today and confirm the biggest lie in the history of Cameroon that he and others told the entire world. He needs not to be afraid. Lapiro is gone and so he should not be frightened. He should come out and stop hiding. If not, he will be haunted by the spirit of Lapiro for the rest of his life. For now, please help me with your thoughts on why Ni John Fru Ndi has been missing in action.

Jacob Nguni

Micro,

In response to your question, I don't know the precise month of the year, but I can tell you that Mimba we was released in 1989 because Lapiro was part of a group of musicians that organized a music concert at the Mateco sports complex in Ngoa-ekelle; wherein he entered the stadium by scaling the fence after giving "choko" of FCFA 200 to one "mbere" who let him in. The gate fee was FCFA 1000. The others were Ndedi Eyango, Gilbraltar Drackus and

Dina Bell. FYI, until the political struggles began, the most thrilling song in that album was "Fogoh ma woh" not even "Mimba we."

Micro, I was a student at the university then, and lived these experiences. I did not hear about them. I have no motivation to be revisionist in my analysis. You seem fixated on your premise that Lapiro was a political kingmaker and Fru Ndi rose to the pinnacle of the political spotlight on Lapiro's tailcoats. And all what I did was to demonstrate to you that your assertion is not borne out by the FACTS. For you or anyone to discount Samuel Eboua, JJ Ekindi, Dicka Akwa, Hameni Bieleu, Mboua Massock Ekani Anicet, Gustave Essaka, Kodock and others and try to elevate Lapiro to the status of Mandela, indeed defies logic.

You should have noticed that when I cite the opposition leaders in Douala at the time, I don't include Fru Ndi on the list, because he played no central role, beyond Bamenda. After the bold act of defiance with the launching of the SDF on May 26, 1990, Biya eventually accepted multiparty and so other parties, including the SDF registered officially. The 1990 Liberty Laws also granted amnesty and people like Bello Bouba came back into the country. Dakolle Daisalla and Issa Tchiroma and others were released from jail. There was widespread popular euphoria and hope for change. I am therefore surprised at the importance you are trying to ascribe to Lapiro; who should ordinarily be a footnote in the history of the struggle.

As for your allegation about Djeukam Tchameni and the so-called attempt to blackmail Lapiro, the public can draw its own conclusions. Lapiro had several opportunities to set the record straight, and he did not at any time made reference to this new story of fabricated millions to discredit him.

That Lapiro was paid to take part in the "concert for peace" is not in doubt because others like Ben Decca, Nkotti Francois were also paid. The problem is that Lapiro's "constituency" thought taking part in a music contest to call for peace was at variance with the objective of "Biya Must Go" and felt betrayed. I was at the *Salle des fêtes* when Lapiro came and was greeted with boos and jeers when he tried to lecture the crowd against violence and vandalism. Then the stones started raining and he had to be whisked out of the venue inside an armored police car.

Micro, a facsimile of the check made out to Lapiro was mischievously leaked to the press with a copy of his ID card when he tried to cash the check. Lapiro has never denied that he was paid because all the musicians who took part in the concert were paid. That concert followed the attempt to burn down Hotel Arcade Tropicana after Immeuble Stamatiades had been razed by arsonists. It was sponsored by SITABAC owned by James Onobiono. So this whole idea of trying to burnish Lapiro's image as a victim of some conspiracy by his "bamileke" brothers is baseless and entirely without merit. When newspapers ran the story, Lapiro used his next album to launch vitriolic attacks against journalists like Pius Njawe (*Le Messager*) and Severin Tchounkeu (*Nouvelle Expression*). But Ndinga Man had lost credibility and the album did not gain traction. What was evident was that the name Lapiro had become synonymous to a sell-out like Epesse.

Lapiro's return as a "garrison commander" in the 2008 uprising was an attempt at self-redemption and his prison sentence was overplayed by the media for propaganda purposes; which earned him international sympathy, but Lapiro was no kingmaker; never was, and never would be. The struggle was started by university students when we marched to launch the SDF in Yaounde after we had gone on strike following the arrest of our lecturers after the famous Cameroon Calling of May 6, 1990. The student Parliament shook the country to its foundation; but just because *Sauveteurs* ran riot during the ghost towns; doesn't make the self-appointed "Complice" a kingmaker. Micro, you failed to prove to me how Lapiro's activities in Douala during the ghost town benefited Fru Ndi and changed his political fortunes. You can do this by telling me what position Lapiro occupied at the time and what specifically he did and how that benefited Fru Ndi.

Ekinneh Agbaw-Ebai

Mr. Owona,

Simply put, you have demonstrated your complete dislike for Lapiro. The above statement like the rest of what you wrote leaves no one with the disdain you must have been treating this once in a life-time hero. I wish you were in Buffalo to listen to the same Celestin Monga you are talking about who said in his Church tribute to Lapiro that it was Lapiro and his fame that rescued him from the claws of your masters.

Going by what Mr. Celestin Monga said, how can you possibly say that Lapiro became known because of the people he used his popularity to have them released? Doesn't that contradict your position? Is it anybody who goes into the street and pulls a crowd to demand that someone be released from jail? Of course not. It takes only a very powerful popular figure like Lapiro to achieve that.

BTW, when was the last time you learnt that any other Cameroonian successfully went out to demand the release of someone? Do you know any other person who ever achieved that in that dungeon known as Cameroon? Give praise to whom it's due. Lapiro was not just anybody, my dear friend.

147

There is nothing you can do about Lapiro's fame that went across the borders of Cameroon to the international scene. Lapiro has addressed international forums that you may never address at any point in your life. I do not know what you mean by "an obscure musician" because while you spend your time talking about Lapiro, Lapiro left this world without knowing that someone like you existed. I wonder how much you can show your disdain for a guy who rose to prominence through personal efforts.

Just accept the fact that you know nothing about Lapiro. You are probably one of those who were hired to spread the rumor that Lapiro had dined and collected money from Jean Fochive. Can you also tell us where that dinner took place? You do not know Lapiro by any stretch. It has always been the focus of people like you to destroy anyone calling the regime in place to order.

And what do you mean by empirical data? Is it like the one that you also submitted to back up your bunch of rumors and outright lies about a man you do not know? I do not need any data to back up that which is evident. Do you need any "empirical" data to prove Obama is president of the USA?

I see you insinuating that Lapiro was probably one of the "bas peuple" because he fought for them. Let me advice you that Fela who sang for the poor did not come from a poor family and was not poor. Likewise, I will like you to investigate Sandjo family. Lapiro's father, Sandjo Roger-Blanchard was a very prominent businessman whose business covered the Mungo area into Kumba where he had a coffee mill. He was a polygamist with 27 children. He was a multi-millionaire.

Pa Sandjo's children lacked nothing and as such do not think that because Lapiro was destined to be a musician means that he was poor by any stretch. Lapiro was born with a golden spoon in the mouth. His father worked hard for his money and had nothing to do with government contracts. Go find out who Lapiro's siblings are PhD, Medical doctors, engineers, architects, etc., you name it and you will find them aplenty in the Sandjo family. Again, you do not know Lapiro beyond the fact that he was a musician.

There is no amount of money that Lapiro could not get from his father. He left all those riches and focused on what God had reserved for him and so, it is an insult for people like you to be talking about this fake 22 million figure and a dinner that never took place just because you feel that such antics will fit into the "low class" statute that musicians in Cameroon have been placed by people who will leave this world as quietly as they came in.

FYI, Lapiro was the highest paid recording artist in Cameroon during the late 80's. He also had a multi-million FCFA contract with SITABAC for the promotion of "Tara" cigarette, which he coined himself. You did/do not know the guy; period. The fact that musicians who operate in Cameroon are treated with all types of disdain should not mislead you to categorize every musician as such.

I know what I am talking about and I have lived these hateful attacks myself. It is one of those things that anyone who is popular at any level should expect. Those of us in this profession know what people like you think of us. But the fact is that little minds will never cease discussing about other people while great minds will forever remain the port of creativity to move the world. I am not against you playing your own role as mandated by your destiny. Destiny may not be altered even as we try to shape our destinies every day.

There is at least one thing that all of us, Christians, owe Judas Iscariot. It is because of his betrayal that Jesus Christ formally proved that He was the son of God. That was the bad but important role that Judas Iscariot had to play without which, the story of Jesus Christ would have been somehow incomplete. So, whatever role you are here on earth to play maybe actually beyond your control. I beg God everyday never to allow me play a bad role at any time.

There might be someone, somewhere, as we speak who is destined to take you down. May be you have not even met that person and that person may not even know you as we speak. But the very events that may actualize what I am saying may come to pass. I am speaking figuratively and so you do not need to take what I am saying out of context to mean that someone is going to take you down. I am simply being philosophical.

I am fine with my position vis-à-vis Lapiro not necessarily because I am a colleague or childhood friend of his but because I have lived in a society where people have been brought down by far more complex plots than what Ndjeukam Tchameni and Co did to Lapiro. They have tried that with me as well at different levels but my Nigerian experience comes in handy to derail such nonsense. And so, please, please, stop spreading lies and false rumors just because for some reason you do not like Lapiro. He is gone now and will cause no more "harm" to anybody's inflated ego.

To end, can you tell me why Ni John Fru Ndi has been quiet since the passing of Lapiro? Whether Lapiro helped him or not is irrelevant to my point. Fru Ndi at least worked very closely with Lapiro who threw his support behind him. So, isn't it a cause for concern that Fru Ndi has not said a word? If you do not know that answer, do not think that some of us do not also know. It is beyond political correctness. And please, do not pretend to defend Fru Ndi because of Lapiro.

Ni Fru Ndi is not your friend and he is the last person you want to see prosper in that country.

PS: The celebration of Lapiro's life is going to happen on May 2, 2014. I am inviting you to mark our calendar and make it to DC. No excuses because you are a constant visitor to the USA. Bring your flowers and gifts and celebrate the life of this great brother with us. The widow will be there. That is my fervent request to you. Do not say that I did not invite you.

Jacob Nguni

Instead of a conclusion, this book ends with an epilogue in which we cast prying eyes on the import of Lapiro de Mbanga's latest musical legacy titled *Démissionnez!*

Chapter 8

Epilogue: Carton rouge de Lapiro à Paul Biya

There is no question that Lapiro's latest single titled *Démissionnez* is a rap on President Paul Biya of Cameroon by a valiant dissident musician who views the Cameroonian leader as undeserving of the public office he holds. Lapiro de Mbanga wears the shoe and knows where it pinches. As this analysis indicates, he resorts to music not only as a medium for expressing his political militancy but also as a tool of resistance. He has been branded Cameroon's version of Fela Anikulapo by friends and foes alike for his oralized dissidence. He has distinguished himself as one who is not afraid to tell those at the helm in Cameroon that they are messing up the country they purport to govern; that their modus operandi has brought more grief than bliss to the Cameroonian people.

Shortly after his release from the New Bell maximum Security prison in Douala where he spent three years on bogus charges, the veteran musician composed a song titled *Démissionnez* or *Step down* in which he urges President Paul Biya to step down from his position as president. According to Lapiro de Mbanga, Biya has failed miserably as president of Cameroon for thirty years and should save face by relinquishing power without fuss. The following review of *Démissionnez* is an attempt at unraveling the leadership conundrum in Cameroon as expressed in Lapiro's latest musical composition.

Démissionnez is Lapiro's last ditch battle with the Biya regime shortly before his death in the United States of America where he lived with his family. Like his mentor, Fela

Anikulapo Kuti, he comes out armed with a volley of aphorisms like this one: 'Ce qui ne tue pas l'homme le rend plus fort/ Un animal blessé doit être achevé sinon gare à toi lorsqu'il va charger (the thing that does not kill you makes you stronger/ a wounded animal must be finished/otherwise woe betide you when he charges) This is probably Lapiro's way of telling President Biya that every dog has its day. In other words, Biya may run but he cannot hide. It is important to underscore the fact that *Démissionnez* is a multi-vocalic piece featuring Valsero, and a bunch of other resilient Cameroonian budding musicians such as Awilo whose defiant voice you hear as follows:

> Lapiro be dong tok all,
> Jess no, yi must kale daso begin nye,
> Yi be dong tory wuna bible,
> Na chapter dis!
> [Lapiro had said it all,
> Right now he only has to sit and observe
> What he has written is the Gospel
> Here is a chapter culled from it!]

What Awilo is saying is that Lapiro had said it all. Right now, all he has to do is sit down and watch events unfold. He claims that Lapiro speaks like the Bible and describes *Démissionnez* as a chapter taken out of the Bible according to St. Lapiro: "Na chapter dis!" In other words, this is a chapter culled from Lapiro's Bible! In typical Mboko style, *Démissionnez* opens with a loud-sounding announcement of Lapiro de Mbanga's return to the musical scene after three years of incarceration:

Ça c'est le grand retour de
Lapiro de Mbanga!
Le Ngata Man!
Vous allez danser aaahhh!
Ça s'annonce!
According to the Bible,
All man must youa ngata!
According to the Church weh
Yi dong be for dis world—
Association des bandits!
This is the big return of
Lapiro de Mbanga!
The Ngata man!
You're going to dance, aaahhh!
This is the beginning!
According to the Bible,
Everyone must go to ngata!
According to the Church which
Which has been created in this world,
Association of bandits!]

Lapiro's song is somewhat prophetic about the fate of the powers-that-be in Cameroon considering the fact that he predicts the eventuality of big shots, including the head of state, incarcerated in the not too distant future: "According to the Bible/All man must youa ngata!" This prophecy is coming true, what with the incarceration in Kondengui of Biya's former ministers like Hamidou Marafa, Ephraim Inoni, Atangana Mebara and Titus Edzoa among others? We cannot gloss over the question of language choice in Lapiro de Mbanga's recent musical composition. The Mboko-type Pidgin English he speaks in this song is remarkably germane with his targeted audience — the rank and file. It is for this reason that the musician opts for a word like "ngata" instead of "la prison." Sauveteurs, bendskinneurs, taximen, feymen, wolowoss and more are prone to using this word in lieu of its more conventional alternative "prison."

To put this differently, Lapiro de Mbanga's diction is in synchrony with the speech mannerisms and patterns of the people whose plight he bemoans in his song. Another striking feature of his diction is language mixing. The stanza above is a mix of French and Pidgin English. A foreigner listening to Lapiro's song may draw a blank and begin to wonder why the singer opts for linguistic pluralism. Lapiro's French becomes less and less standardized as he continually draws from several local registers. He effectively uses the interplay of several codes — standard French, Pidgin English, and indigenous languages —as an artistic device for not only foregrounding the idiosyncrasies of his compatriots but also for evaluating their relationships to one another. This leads us to the conclusion that *Démissionnez* is a hybridized song that requires listeners to be not just bilingual but also multilingual in order to successfully unravel the latent meanings embedded in the singer's lexical choices. This study enables us to appreciate not just the particular importance the songwriter attaches to linguistic innovation as an artistic device but also the cultural hybridity that serves as the substructure on which the song is composed. This entire album is woven around a soccer metaphor in which Lapiro attributes to President Biya the triple roles of selector, coach and captain:

Na you be sélectionneur, coach and capitaine joueur,
Na you di mek classement for ndamba,
Na you be préparateur physique, soignant
Ana na you be alamigu for da you own sia Manchester.

[You're the team leader, coach and captain,
You plan soccer marches
You groom players physically and
And the alpha and omega of your
Simulacrum Manchester team]

However, no sooner has he painted Biya as a leader who tries to multi-task than he starts to blast him on his monumental shortcomings as this except suggests:

Trente ans de championnats
You dong composé équipes
Wuna dong buka ndamba for all kain kain stade…
Sep so, soso défaites because of over boum! Boum!
Kondre man, ndamba no be boum! Boum!
Ndamba na sense!
Ndamba na sense ancien répé
No be na boum! Boum!
Ndamba na sense ancien répé,
No be tchouquer! Tchouquer!
[Thirty years of championships
You have formed team upon team
Your teams have played matches in all kinds of stadia…
Even then, all you can show is a series lost matches
On account of excessive boum! Boum!
Compatriot, soccer is not boum! Boum!
Soccer is intelligence!
Soccer is intelligence old répé
It is not boum! Boum!
Soccer is intelligence old répé
It is not chuk! Chuk!]

There is no question that *Démissionnez* is a rap on the government of President Biya by a valiant musician who views the Cameroonian leader as undeserving of the public office he holds. It is for this reason that Lapiro does not mince words in calling upon Biya to do the right thing by stepping down in the following excerpt:

Démissionnez! Démissionnez!
Démissionnez! Démissionnez!
Ils ont été dépassés-eh!
Ils ont voulu libérer-eh!
J'ai refusé; j'ai ndem les bêtises!
Lapiro! Lapiro! Lapiro!
The very, very!
[Step down! Step down!
Step down! Step down!
They were overwhelmed!
They had wanted to release him-eh!
I refused; I shoved their nonsense aside!
Lapiro! Lapiro! Lapiro!
The very, very!]

As Lapiro sees it, soccer teams lose because their captains are inept. By the same token, he puts the blame for the retrogression of Cameroon on the shoulders of Paul Biya, the team captain, as the lyrics in the following excerpt suggest:

If joueurs dem di mouiller-oh
Leke na coach go pay!
If youa équipe ndima, ndima–oh!
Leke na coach musi go!
If youa joueurs dem di njoum, njoum-oh!
Like na coach dem go massacrer.

158

If youa équipe na soso défaite-oh!
If youa joueurs dem di mouiller-oh,
Leke na you musi go!
If youa équipe na distributeur des points-oh!
If youa joueurs dem na loss sense-oh!
Leke na you dem go massacrer.
Loss sense!

Lapiro chooses his words very carefully in a bid to transmit important messages to his audience as seen in the foregoing lampoon on Biya's ineptitude and dismal failure in statecraft. The songwriter believes that the problem with Cameroon lies with its leaders. Leadership crises have produced the skeletal Cameroonian nation that the world has become accustomed to nowadays. Yet President Biya and his cohorts make believe that there is nothing wrong with Cameroon. Lapiro finds this governmental half-truth irksome and deems it necessary to denounce as follows:

You fall for ngombe...
You mek leke say you no ba yia.
You give me da coup de tête weh
You be take sissia Eric Chinje because
You be get ma macabo since yia ba yia.
And how I dong go bata moua
You nye for da affaire for constipation for constitution,
You dong profité for émeutes 2008
You send tapi for ma sai,
I go boulot njo ngata for three yia,
I bambe chaîne, ana I nang for cédé.

This song harbors seeds of a revolution judging by the defiant tone of the songwriter. It is also a remembrance of

159

some interesting historical moments in Cameroon. Lapiro takes listeners on a walk down memory lane. Cameroonians would recall that many years ago, Mr. Biya, in his usual cavalier manner, told Cameroon's ace journalist, Eric Chinje, during an interview that he could be fired based on nothing but the whims and caprices of the head of state. This threat will be remembered by most Cameroonians living at the time as "le coup de tête du Président Biya", which could be translated as "President Biya's nod." Another historical event that is referenced in this song is the 2008 uprisings in the major cities of Cameroon. Lapiro de Mbanga flexes his muscles energetically as he wags his symbolic finger in the face of President Paul Biya, as these lines indicate:

> Donc you musi sabi sei popo you
> You dong chercha and you dong trouva
> And you musi supporta!
> For da supporta, you musi tie heart
> You chop maîtrise because say,
> Conformément à l'article 19
> For la Charte internationale
> Des droits de l'homme,
> Ana according to the motion de soutien
> Ana appel du peuple way ma complice dem
> Dong geep me, I go spit fire jess now leke dragon,
> Kwaah!

It is interesting how Lapiro resorts to figures of speech such as similes to elevate himself above the level of the ordinary Cameroonian. When he equates his diatribes against Biya to the fire-spitting of a dragon, it becomes self-evident that Lapiro situates himself in the realm of the superhuman.

It is for this same reason that he hyperbolically describes his vendetta against the Beti-led regime in Yaounde as a tsunami :

Na tsunami I di déclencher for dis heure
I no geep kong l'heure!
Popo me I sabi say dis tour
No be na ngata again,
Na for deme me en direct
Ana I day prêt for meng.

Words of defiance, indeed! Lapiro makes it abundantly clear that he is not scared by death. In fact, he says he is ready to lay down his life for the common good: "Ana I day prêt for meng." He further points out that he has sworn to wage the war against corruption in Cameroon from time immemorial:

De toutes les façons
I be dong prêté serment from yia by yia say
I go domo, donc camarade combattant Pius Njawe
Maître Mbami Augustin
A luta continua!

Lapiro's declaration of war against the cancerous regime of Paul Biya is ominous: "A luta continua!" This resonates with the attitude of a defying indefatigable combatant primed to do battle with adversaries till doomsday. The football metaphor used by Lapiro constitutes the single most effective trope he employs to cast aspersions on the lame duck government of Paul Biya, a man held in contempt by the generality of Cameroonians. It is interesting to note that Lapiro brings the head of state from the pedestal of his ivory tower to the level of the rank and file. Listen to the manner in which Lapiro addresses the president:

I say hein wuoh, dat équipe for Lions domptables
Wei you dong nuong for Besie for Kondengui
Ana for Besie for New Bell
Wei na popo you dong formé yi,
Yes, na you be Sah for da équipe
Nationale de shiba
Na you di recruiter joueurs
And na you di make dem licenses.
Na you be sélectionneur,
Coach and capitaine joueur,
Na you di make classement for ndamba.

This stylistic device may not make sense to folks who do not understand the game of soccer. However, Lapiro's recourse to soccer metaphor makes perfect sense to the people of Cameroon for whom football has become a national 'religion' of sorts. It should be noted that the word "wuoh" called from the native tongues of the grasslands people in the Northwest Region translates to a relationship of camaraderie. However, used derogatorily as Lapiro does in this song, the word takes on a different signification—one of contempt. Lapiro lambastes the Cameroonian Head of State for his predilection for power monopoly: "Na you be sélectionneur/Coach ana Capitaine joueur/Na you di make classement for ndamba". In other words, Paul Biya is the selector, coach and capitan. He sorts out players for matches which often result in defeat! It is on this count that Lapiro describes Biya's team as "youa own sia Manchester." He reminds the president that for thirty years he has been unable to win a single match:

Trente ans de championnats
You dong composé équipes
Wuna dong boka ndamba for all kain stade
Sep so soso défaite because of over boum! boum!
Kondre man, ndamba no be boum! boum!
Ndamba na sense!
Ndamba na sense, ancien répé
No be na boum! Boum!

Lapiro's intent is to draw the attention of the public to Biya's usurpation of power from the judicial and legislative branches of government in Cameroon. Biya has silenced Cameroon's judges and Members of Parliament who remain at his beck and call as the following lines indicate:

For règlement intérieur for you démocratie avancée à grande vitesse
Pouvoir exécutif, pouvoir judiciaire ana pouvoir législatif
Na you di flotter; sotai you dong take Président for Assemblée Nationale you make garçon de courses way you di commissionner
For say yi go représenter you mbout événements for nassah pays dem.

Undaunted as ever, the defiant musician does not mince words in calling upon the Cameroonian head of state to step down because he has not only failed the Cameroonian people but has also tinkered with the national constitution abusively in order to stay in power in perpetuity:

Step down! Démissionnez!
Because you dong over massacré constitution…
You dong over échouer

Subordination for pouvoir judiciaire
Way politique di manoeuvrer witi ingérence
For inside décisions for justice...
Ana na soso witi da hanhan
You be make me I youa ngata sotai for las heure
Nations Unies commot lookam ton rouge forseka Ndinga
Man...

Lapiro argues in his lyrics that suppression of the
judiciary by the executive branch of government has resulted
in manipulation and interference by the executive branch in
the interpretation of the letter and spirit of the law. It is clear
that abuse of power is the leitmotif that runs through Lapiro's
songwriting. The singer bemoans the sad fate of his
compatriots who have to live in perpetual fear on account of
generalized insecurity as the following lines seem to suggest:

Insécurité généralisée
De ngenge dong hala for banque for Bonaberi
De ngenge dong hala for Pont de Wouri
Dem dong massacré you représentant
Chef de terre, Monsieur le sous-préfet ana Kamabourou
for Bakassi
You dong over mouiller!

Unlike some myopic Cameroonians who believe that Paul
Biya is a godsend for his people, Lapiro curses the stars that
saddled his fatherland with this human albatross on that
fateful day of November 6, 1982! His handiwork spells doom
for all Cameroonians, Francophones and Anglophones alike:

Privatisations sauvage for produits toxiques
For société des mbokube way di gee pipo cancer...

Milito and sous-officiers dem dong ton watch nite
For microfinances dem di catch for before long
For ndoh weti cutlass for hand
Braconniers dem di massacrer we phone for mboko
Chop chair for SONEL ana SNEC dem di soso sap
quittances
Dem di take ndoh; lumière witi ndiba no day.
Sapeurs pompiers dong ton SNEC
Sotai na dem di sap ndiba
Yes, na fire brigade dem di sap stone for yong for Ngola.

Lapiro tells it like it is; no beating around the bush! These
lines are satirical. Public utilities are in a state of dysfunction
in Cameroon. The electricity company code-named SNEC,
sends out bills to clients who have been living in darkness for
months! The water distributor, SNEC, does not fare any
better as the following lines seem to suggest: "Chop chair for
SONEL ana SNEC dem di soso sap quittances / Dem di take
ndoh, lumière witi ndiba no dei." This is utter dereliction of
duty on the part of public officials on whom it is incumbent
to ascertain that citizens are treated humanely and given their
money's worth!

As it is customary in Cameroon, state officials like
ministers turn a blind eye to wanton abuse of power:

Ministre for Santé de kop nye
For da cholera way dem di sapam for pipo
Yi di wait taim way dem go sauter yi for Kondengui
Before yi begin publier yi own lettre ouverte for Bra sei:
'J'avais dit que, j'avais fait que
Je voulais même démissionner, so na so.'
Popo you, you go begin hala say:
'Woyoh! Ma woyoh! Ma woyoh!'

Wosai ndiba go commot for mouf you for dang fire?

It should be noted that Lapiro is deriding former Minister Hamidou Marafa who did not read the handwriting on the wall and waited until his boss, Pa Paul, dumped him at the Kondengui Maximum Security Prison in Yaounde. Marafa is noted for having reacted to his arrest and incarceration by writing a series of weekly letters from his prison cell in an attempt to assuage the wrath of the Lord Mayor of Etoudi. But it was too late! In a word, Lapiro is laughing tongue-in-cheek at those Cameroonians who create carnivorous systems that devour its own creators. Lapiro cautions Cameroonian ministers who still have closets full of skeletons to make hay while the sun shines. They should resign without further ado before the axe falls on them.

Lapiro's "Démissionnez" is a discourse on the fate of Cameroon's socially marginalized. He bemoans the lot of the so-called 'lost generation', or Paul Biya's fodder for cannon. Hear what their spokesman has to say about them:

Foreseka over ngeme and chômage
Way yi dong multiplié for dis mboko
Bendskinneurs, chauffeurs clando,
Laveurs de voitures, tackleurs, sauveteurs
Bayam sellams, coiffeurs and coiffeuses ambulantes
For Marché Central, call-boxeurs...
Dem di pointer na for dong rain and for dong sun...
Preuve, dem di kick mberi bébés for maternité for side by side
No be you boulot na sécurisation
Des personnes et de leurs biens?
A vrai dire da wan na échouation totale
If you no fit garantir sécurité sep for nourrissons!

166

What Lapiro says in his song is so true that one is simply overcome by joy and inner satisfaction. It is nice to have warriors like him who exert their influence on the goings-on in the homeland using the guitar. Of course, detractors will always rear their ugly heads to denounce an indefatigable combatant like Lapiro de Mbanga but the fact of the matter is that honest people will glean some truth from what he says in his lyrics. Who would deny the fact the primordial duty of a Head of State is the security of his own people? Yet, in Cameroon, we have a President who is absent both physically and psychologically from the land. He does not even know the people he governs, much less care about their daily safety. President Paul Biya did not utter a word when Yaounde was rocked to its very foundation by the inexplicable disappearance of Vanessa Tchatchou's newborn from the Gynaeco-Obsteric and Paediatric Hospital in Ngoussou, Yaounde in 2011. Although there is no evidence to suggest that the State is directly responsible for the disappearance of Vanessa's baby, Cameroon, a signatory of the United Nations Convention on the Rights of the Child, has a legal obligation to protect its babies and uphold their rights. That is the point Lapiro is making when he says: "Preuve, dem di kick mberi bébés for maternité for side by side/ No be you boulot na sécurisation/Des personnes et de leurs biens?"

In other words, babies are being stolen from maternity wards everywhere in Cameroon but the Head of State and his ministers have remained silent. Lapiro's rhetorical question, "No be you boulot na sécurisation/Des personnes et de leurs biens? has fallen on deaf ears given that Paul Biya hides behind the mask of taciturnity to treat Cameroonians like dirt. He is callous, supercilious and indifferent to the plight of his compatriots. To think that this fellow is an ex-seminarian beats everyone's imagination!

Another sore point that Lapiro raises in the excerpt above is the question of chronic joblessness that has transformed Cameroonians into "beasts of no nation", to borrow from Bate Besong (1990), another victim of Biya's villainy: "Foreseka over ngeme and chômage/Way yi dong multiplié for dis mboko. We now have a crop of Cameroonians at home and in the diaspora who are prepared to do whatever it takes to make money, including shedding human blood and selling human remains. Cameroon is replete with feymen (or conmen) who are ruthless in their acts of swindling and robbery. Clouds of insecurity hang in the horizon in Cameroon. You have to be suffering from selective amnesia to deny these facts. It is on this count that Lapiro gives Paul Biya a vote of no confidence on his performance as Head of State for 30years: "A vrai dire da wan na échouation totale." Based on this lamentably poor performance, Lapiro calls on his compatriots to give Paul Biya a vote of no confidence as well; he calls on Cameroon's lame duck President to step down without further ado:

> Popo you répé sep sep dong rétrogradé you
> Say you be daso nomdi, you dong électrocuter Code électoral
> Terminator des terminators!
> You dong make kan kan classement
> Kan kan remplacement
> Sep so, soso défaite sur défaite
> Donc, no be daso faute for joueurs!
> Popo you sep you no well
> You musi lep brassa you step down
> Dat be say you démissionner
> Leke you répé, Grand Camarade
> Way yi been ndash you chia,

Ana wei you dong abandonné for Dakar!

Lapiro masters events that constitute the checkered history of his native land. He uses this knowledge to compose marketable musical stuff. There is no gainsaying the fact that the resignation and eventual death of Cameroon's pioneer president, Ahmadou Ahidjo, in Senegal and Biya's categorical refusal to repatriate his remains constitute a sensitive issue for Cameroonian politicians. But Lapiro believes that this important national problem cannot be swept under the carpet. Younger Cameroonians deserve to know what transpired before the advent of Paul Biya to Etoudi. Lapiro tries to provide them with this knowledge in *Démissionnez*. He reminds Paul Biya that the people of Cameroon 'voted' him into office to do work: "Dem dong voté you na for say you gérer." In my opinion, the word "voter" should be replaced with "voler" because this later word collocates with electoral fraud and gerrymandering that has become the stock-in-trade of the Biya regime. Paul Biya has kept himself in power for thirty years by having recourse to vote rigging.

Lapiro ends *Démissionnez* by having recourse to scatology. The trope of defecation is used abundantly by the musician as a trope to describe Cameroon as a nation in the throes of moral and physical putrefaction:

You know say if person dammer yi musi motoh…
Sabi say you motoh go beaucoup
Ana yi go over noum
Yes ancien chaud gars
Dat be say you go shit
Over big shit ana yi go smell, hmmm!

What an apocalyptic way to end a song pregnant with meaning! There is no running away from it, Cameroon seen through the eyes of Lapiro de Mbanga is a land poised on the edge of a dangerous precipice. Indeed, Cameroon about which he sings is a country tottering on the brink of annihilation, be it piece-meal. Lapiro reminds Cameroon's ship captain that he is living in fool's paradise. He further warns Cameroonians that Biya's self-delusion harbors seeds of calamity of seismic proportions. Yet Paul Biya continues to deny even the obvious:

> You dong las nye da preuves
> Way you be been axam say où sont les preuves?
> For taim way you dong yia
> Say J11 and Brutus Dem di keke you

Sad news indeed, not just for the people of Cameroon but also for Paul Biya himself whom Lapiro perceives as a potential culprit facing possible trial at the International Court of Justice:

> Gendarmes dem for Brettons Woods
> Dem go signer you mandat d'arrêt international
> Because you know say if person dammer yi musi motoh…

To put this differently, on the day of reckoning Paul Biya will be arrested and charged for crimes against humanity. He will be called upon to answer questions on the roles he played or failed to play as the leader of Cameroon for more than thirty traumatic years.

Works cited

Abraham, Roger D. *African-American Literary Criticism, 1773 to 2000*. Ed. Hazel Arnett Ervin. New York: Twayne Publishers, 1999.

Bell, Bernard W. *The Afro-American Novel and its Traditions*. Amherst. University of Massachusetts Press, 1987.

Besong, Bate. *Three Plays*. Yaounde: Editions CLE, 2003.

—————————. *Change Waka & His Man Sawa Boy*. Yaounde: Editions CLE, 2001.

—————————. *The Banquet*. Makurdi: Editions EHI, 1994.

—————————. *Requiem for the Last Kaiser: A Drama of Conscientization and Revolution*. Calabar: Centaur Publishers, 1991.

—————————. *Beasts of No Nation: A Docu-Drama*.Limbe: Nooremac Press, 1990.

—————————.*The Most Cruel Death of the Talkative Zombie: A Faery Play in Three Parts with Revelry at a Requiem*. Limbe: Nooremac Press, 1986.

Campbell, Horace. *Rasta and Resistance: From Marcus Garvey to Walter Rodney*. Trenton: Africa World Press, Inc., 2001.

Ewané, L. M. 1989. "Le Camfranglais, Un cousin du Verlan?" *Afrique Elite* 36, (1989):18-19.

Fanon, Frantz. *The Wretched of the Earth*. Trans.Constance Farrington. New York: Grove Press, 1966.

Gates, Henry Louis, Jr. *The Signifying Monkey: A Theory of African-American Literary Criticism*. New York and Oxford: Oxford University Press, 1989.

Halliday, M.A.K. *Language as a Social Semiotic: The Special Interpretation of Language and Meaning.* Baltimore, University Park Press, 1977.

Hesch, Rick. "Music of Oppression, Music of Resistance," Retrieved January 7, 2007 from http://canadiandimension.com/articles/1805

Julien, Eileen. *African Novels and the question of Orality:* Bloomington: Indiana University Press, 1992.

Kouega, Jean-Paul. (2003): "Camfranglais: A New Slang in Cameroon Schools." *English Today* 19.2, 23–29.

_____. Camfranglais: *A Glossary of Common Words, Phrases and Usages.* Muenchem: LINCOM EUROPA, 2013.

_____. "The Slang of Anglophone Cameroonian University Adolescents." *A Glossary. Syllabus* 1(2010a): 88-116.

_____.Campus English: Lexical Variations in Cameroon." *International Journal of the Sociology of Language,* 199. (2009a): 89-101.

_____. *A Dictionary of Cameroon Pidgin English Usage: Pronunciation, Grammar, and Vocabulary. Muenchem: LINCOM EUROPA,* 2008.

_____. *A Dictionary of Cameroon English Usage.* Berne: Peter Lang, 2007.

_____. *Aspects of Cameroon English Usage: A Lexical Appraisal.* Muenchem: LINCOM EUROPA, 2006.

_____. (2003): "Word formative processes in Camfranglais," *World Englishes* 22-4(2003): 511-539.

_____ (2003): "Camfranglais: A novel slang in Cameroon schools," *English Today* 19-2(2003): 23-29.

_____. "Uses of English in Southern British Cameroons." *World Englishes* 23.1(2002):93-113.

_____. "Pidgin Facing Death in Cameroon." *Terralingua. Retrieved on February 15, 2014 from* http://www.terralingua.org

Mandela, Nelson. *Long Walk to Freedom*. Boston: Back Bay Books, 1994.

Mbuli, Mzwakhe. *Resistance is Defense*. Beverly Hills, Caroline Records, 1992.

Nyamnjoh, Francis and Jude Fokwang. "Entertaining Repression: Music and Politics in Postcolonial Cameroon," *African Affairs* 104/415,(2005): 251-274.

Ong, Walter. *The Presence of the Word*. Minneapolis: University of Minnesota Press, 1981.

_____.*Orality and Literacy: The Technologizing of the Word*. London and New York: Routledge, 1982.

Pareles, Jon. "Fela! Broadway? Dance?" Retrieved October 25, 2010 from http://www.nytimes.com/2009/11/22/theater/22fela.html

Pigeaud, Fanny. (2001). *Au Cameroun de Paul Biya*. Paris: Karthala.

Scheub, Harold. "The Technique of the Expansible Image in Xhosa Ntsomi-Performances." *Research in African Literatures* 1 (1970): 119-146.

_____. "Translation of African Oral Narrative Performance to the Written Word." *Yearbook of Comparative and General Literature*. (1971): 28-36.

_____. "The Art of Nongenile Mazithathu Zenani, a Gcaleka Ntsomi Performer." Ed. Richard Dorson. *African Forklore*. New York: Doubleday, 1972.

_____. *The Xhosa Ntsomi*. Oxford: Clarendon Press, 1975.

_____. "A Review of African Oral Traditions and Literature." *African Studies Review* 28.2-*3* (1985): 1-72.

_____. *The Poem in the Story: Music, Poetry, and Narrative*. Madison: University of Wisconsin Press, 2002.

Solaar, M.C. "La belle et le bad boy," Retrieved March 29, 2014 from http://www.youtube.com/watch?v=T-yK_5IOEHI

_____. "Bouge de là!" Retrieved January 12, 2014 from http://www.youtube.com/watch?v=pqMiEmZ2kOw

Sone, Mirabeau Enongene. (2009). "Lapiro de Mbanaga and Political Vision in Contemporary Cameroon." *The International Journal of Language, Society and Culture* 27, 18-26. http://www.nytimes.com/2009/11/22/theater/22fela.html

Tayannah, Lee McQuillar and Fred Johnson. 2010. *Tupac Shakur: The Life and Times of an American Icon*. Cambridge: Dacapo Press, Thompson, Christopher. 2007. "Mixing Music and Politics in Africa." Retrieved November 4, 2010 from http://www.time.com/time/arts/article/0'8599,1658765,00.html

Vakunta, Peter W. *Ngata Man: Tribute to a Fallen Hero (Lapiro de Mbanga)*. Kindle Edition. Amazon Digital Services, Inc., 2014.

_____.*From Pidgin to Camfranglais: The Making of a New Language in Cameroon*. Kindle Edition. Amazon Digital Services, Inc., 2014.

_____. *Fossoyers des états bananiers*. Kindle Edition. Amazon Digital Services, Inc., 2014.

_____. *Carnet d'un retour au pays natal en camfranglais*. Kindle Edition. Amazon Digital Services, Inc., 2014.

_____. *Bate Besong: Why the Caged Bird Sings*. Kindle Edition. Amazon Digital Services, Inc., 2013.

_____. *Méditations poétiques en camfranglais*. Kindle Edition. Amazon Digital Services, Inc., 2013.

_____. *Speak Camfranglais pour un renouveau Ongolais:* Bamenda: Langaa RPCIG, 2013.

_____. *Ntarikon: Where Rainstorms Gather*. Kindle Edition. Amazon Digital Services, Inc., 2013.

_____. "Demissionnez!" A Call for President Biya to Step Down: A Review of Lapiro's Latest Musical Composition." *Pambazuka* 612(2013):1-9.

_____. *Carton Rouge à Paul Biya, Président de la République du Cameroun: Lapiro's Songs of Protest* (Vol. 1). Kindle Edition, Amazon Digital Services, Inc., 2012.

_____. *A Nation at Risk: A Personal Narrative of the Cameroonian Crisis*. Bloomington: I-Universe, 2012.

_____. "Lapiro in His Own Words: An Interview with Dr. Peter Vakunta," Retrieved August 5, 2012 from http://www.postnewsline.com/2012/08/lapiro-de-mbanga-in-his-own-words-an-interview-with-dr-peter-vakunta.html

_____. "Dr. Peter Wuteh Vakunta's Conversations with Lapiro de Mbanga," Retrieved August 3, 2012 from http://www.youtube.com/watch?v=6QEqwOAklU0

_____. "Lapiro's Musings on President Paul Biya and His CPDM Regime: Tête-à-tête with Dr. Peter Vakunta," September 9, 2012 from http://www.panafricamusicshow.com/2012/09/pam-literature-lapiros-musings-on.html

_____. *Martyrdom and Other Freedom Poems*. Bloomington: I-Universe, 2010.

_____. *Majunga Tok: Poems in Pidgin English*. Bamenda: Langaa RPCIG, 2008.

_____. *Ntarikon: Poetry for the Downtrodden*. Bloomington: Author House, 2008.

_____. *Cry My Beloved Africa: Essays on the Postcolonial Aura in Africa*. Bamenda: Langaa RPCIG, 2008.

_____. *Paradise of Idiots: Poetry*. Bloomington: Author House, 2008.

Verschave, François Xavier. *De la Françafrique à la Mafiafrique*. Bruxelles: Editions Tribord, 2004.

Zabus, Chantal. The African Palimpsest: Indigenization of Language in the West African Europhone Novel. Amsterdam: Rodopi, 1991.

Ze Amvela, Etienne. (1989.) "Reflexions on the Social Implications of Bilingualism in the Republic of Cameroon." Annals of the Faculty of Letters and Social Sciences. Yaoundé: University of Yaounde.

Discography

Lapiro, de Mbanga. *Démissionnez!* Retrieved August 10, 2012 from http://www.youtube.com/watch?v=v5xy2xg9774

_____. "Lef am so," Retrieved August 15, 2009 from http://www.youtube.com/watch?v=LVYEAs-OtXM

_____."Constitution constipée," Retrieved June 19, 2010 from

_____.

http://www.youtube.com/watch?v=LVYEAs-OtXM

_____. "Na You,"Retrieved August 15, 2008 from http://www.youtube.com/watch?v=Thqb_aTByAE)

_____. "Kop nie," Retrieved September 21, 2010 from http://www.youtube.com/watch?v=Thqb_aTByAE)

_____."Mimba wi," Retrieved September 16 http://www.youtube.com/watch?v=Thqb_aTByAE

_____. "Pas argent pas amour," Retrieved July 18, Retrieved September 21, 2010 from http://www.youtube.com/watch?v=Thqb_aTB

_____."Qui n'est rien n'a rien," Retrieved September 21, 2010 from http://www.youtube.com/watch?v=Thqb_aTB

_____. "Jolie fille," Retrieved July 18, Retrieved September 21, 2010 from http://www.youtube.com/watch?v=Thqb_aTB

_____."Mi nding mi be, foua." Retrieved July 18, Retrieved September 21, 2010 from http://www.youtube.com/watch?v=Thqb_aTB

_____. "Overdone," Retrieved November 12, 20122 http://www.youtube.com/watch?v=pzBbHqhLQi0

_____. "Nak Pasi," Retrieved March 17, 2014 from http://www.youtube.com/watch?v=hasn-1BPFfk

_____. "Na wou go pay?" Retrieved April 2, 2014 fromhttp://www.youtube.com/watch?v=_aB_luGtXG8

_____. "No woman no cry," Retrieved March 12, 2013 from http://www.youtube.com/watch?v=Zkicp8KsWLM

_____. "Fogwa ma wo," Retrieved April 3, 2014 from http://www.youtube.com/watch?v=fz7xISSewvQ

_____. "No make erreur," Retrieved April 1, 2014 http://www.youtube.com/watch?v=Qkb4LihLfY8

_____. "Dem se" Retrieved January 23, 2012 http://www.youtube.com/watch?v=hcrAo0mz_AA

_____. "Qui n'a rien n'a rien," Retrieved April 4, 2014 from http://www.youtube.com/watch?v=ru-1gcyxeSI

_____. "Jolie filles," Retrieved December 12, 2011 from http://www.youtube.com/watch?v=j-nYUO8IMzU

_____. "Bayam Sellam" Retrieved October 12, 2013 from http://www.youtube.com/watch?v=FsJ54dMJPKM

_____. "Foua Foua" Retrieved December 30 2013 from http://www.youtube.com/watch?v=ibg6rl3MNEQ

_____. "Souviens-toi chéri," Retrieved March 12, 2000 from http://www.youtube.com/watch?v=OjCJNyY2-gw

Danny Elwood. "Mon cousin militaire," Retrieved November 20, 2007 from http://www.youtube.com/watch?v=d5R16Z5Xtfc

_____. "Je suis Pygmée," Retrieved April 26, 2010 from http://www.youtube.com/watch?v=ttRzfODcAXw

_____. "En haut," Retrieved July9, 2007 from http://www.youtube.com/watch?v=36LZMUmPucE

_____."Mon chien Dick Dick Dick," Retrieved 29, 2007 from http://www.youtube.com/watch?v=mjh-fDhNfD4

_____. "Turlupiner," Retrieved July, 2007 from http://www.youtube.com/watch?v=j0ybo7MER-E

_____. "Akao Manga," Retrieved July 22, 2010 from http://www.youtube.com/watch?v=R7SuYydcNGY

_____. "Odontol," Retrieved July 14, 2009 from http://www.youtube.com/watch?v=uZrk14mSvhc

_____. "Je t'aimais, je t'aime, t'aimerai," June 14, 2012 from http://www.youtube.com/watch?v=CLilVeKzJRs

179

Valsero a.k.a Le Général. "Lettre au président," Retrieved May 11, 2009 from http://www.youtube.com/watch?v=a28WhRWrrx4

_____. "Ce pays tue les jeunes," Retrieved January 26, 2009 from http://www.youtube.com/watch?v=Z4XJDegyuYE

_____. "Réponse du président à Valsero" Retrieved March 30, 2012 from http://www.youtube.com/watch?v=ys-xf3cLPX0

_____. "Valsero répond," Retrieved December 27, 2009 from http://www.youtube.com/watch?v=cBuPpx1KmQo

_____. "Valsero, ne me parle pas du Cameroun," Retrieved March 22, 2009 from http://www.youtube.com/watch?v=siGRwpgvliY

_____. "Holdup," Retrieved July 7, 2010 from http://www.youtube.com/watch?v=14UEWJ_TGhI

_____. "Va voter," Retrieved February 7, 2010 from http://www.youtube.com/watch?v=BwRYZkD3JYU

_____. "3e lettre au président," Retrieved September 28, 2011 from http://www.youtube.com/watch?v=A_qo8l9oCcA

_____. "Femme seule," Retrieved November 8, 2012 from http://www.youtube.com/watch?v=7-aB5b89Tek

_____. "Quitte les choses," October 5, 2012 from http://www.youtube.com/watch?v=77pMLUquBfk

_____. "Je porte plainte," Retrieved June 2, 2013 from http://www.youtube.com/watch?v=14H2onzcFEI

_____. Le langage des armes," Retrieved December 6, 2012 from http://www.youtube.com/watch?v=dlaBXHDyN5g

Index

Kumba 19, 23, 36, 39, 89, 120, 140, 148

L
Lagos 28
Lapiro 12, 14, 15, 16, 17, 18, 20, 23, 24, 28, 29, 30, 31, 33, 35, 39, 40, 50, 53, 55, 62
Lapiro de Mbanga 17, 170
Lapirioism 57, 69, 71, 87, 92, 94, 98, 134
Liberia 21, 37
Literacy 2, 3, 173
Literature 13
Lion Man 81, 82
Lobé 42, 62
Longué Longué 42

M
Makossa 88, 89, 108
Malinké 1
Mamba 6
Mandela 9, 26, 59, 145, 173
Marafa 99, 100, 155, 165
Martine Luther King 25, 47
Mbanga 12, 14, 15, 17, 18, 20, 24, 26, 30, 31, 35, 39, 41, 42, 52, 86
Mbuli 43, 173
Moni Bile 64
Muna 13, 29, 97, 123
Mungo 19, 36, 68, 148

N
Nchinda 58, 64, 101
Ndam Njoya 13, 18, 29, 34, 100, 134, 136
Ndamba 5, 97, 156, 157, 162-3

W

Wanda 95, 98, 99, 101, 104
Woyoh 165

Y

Yaounde 29, 119
Yoruba 37
Youth Talk 88

Z

Zabus 65, 176
Ze Amvela 44, 176
Zongang 13, 29
Zuma 22